Hidden Wealth:
The Money Making Power of Licensing

A Step-by-Step Guide
to Making Money with Intellectual Property

By Rand Brenner
President & CEO
Licensing Consulting Group

Hidden Wealth: The Money Making Power of Licensing

A Step-by-Step Guide
to Making Money with Intellectual Property

Copyright © 2019 Rand Brenner

First paperback edition July 2019

ISBN 978-0-578-53604-0 (paperback)

Published by Hidden Wealth Books
www.hiddenwealthbooks.com

Contents

CHAPTER 1

Why Licensing?

What if you could generate income without making, marketing, or selling anything? Well, you can. I'm going to share with you information on one of today's most significant money-making assets on the planet - bigger than real estate, stock, bonds, and precious metals - yet very few people understand it. It is the wealth creator of the 21st century. Most of the wealthiest people in the world have used this wealth-creating asset to build some of the biggest fortunes of the last decade. Creating wealth with this asset doesn't need any experience or money. And you don't have to own anything.

I have a lifetime of experience making money with this asset. What is this wealth creating opportunity? It's called intellectual property, and I'm going to tell you how to create wealth - lots of wealth - licensing intellectual property.

You don't have to own intellectual property to make money with it. As an agent or deal finder, you help IP owners license their IP to third-party marketers and get paid a commission. Or you can acquire the master licensing rights to an IP, sub-license it to other companies and make money from the royalties paid by the sub-licensees to the IP owner.

Hidden Wealth: The Money Making Power of Licensing

There are also opportunities to find intellectual property owners with unused or old IP that when combined with other IP, can create a new IP licensing opportunity. For example, you could find some IP owners that have unused consumer products or software that's bundled and licensed into new distribution channels or territories.

Licensing is one of the easiest and fastest ways for generating revenue with intellectual property assets. Licensing lets you tap into companies who already have the wheel in motion. It's a quicker, cheaper, and less risky way to make money with your IP.

A Global Multi-Billion-Dollar Business

Licensing is a multi-billion-dollar global business. Nobody knows for sure how big it is, but it continues to grow every year. Intellectual property laws are maturing around the world as countries recognize the tremendous economic importance of IP. The licensing process is the same almost everywhere in the world. You can use it to expand internationally, or find new and exciting IP to launch in your home county.

Just about every industry today uses licensing - consumer and business products, technology, healthcare, pharmaceuticals, electronics, and more. Services and know-how of all types are also being licensed, including marketing systems, educational programs, corporate training methods, human resource development, and a host of other know-how IP created by professional service providers.

Many companies recognize that the more others build upon their IP, the bigger their market grows. A good example is a brand licensing. This strategy enables companies with well-known brands to use that recognition value and take advantage of the demand for non-competitive products.

What Is Licensing?

Licensing is a process. It includes a vocabulary - the language of licensing; a procedure - a way of thinking and doing; and a transaction - an agreement that creates value and makes money.

Licensing is like buying and selling real estate. Like real estate, it leverages the equity "value" of your IP. However, instead of burdening it with debt, you build your IP value every by using it in the marketplace. But unlike real estate (which can only be used by one renter), your IP is an abundant property that many partners can use simultaneously. And that's what creates big money from your IP.

But licensing is more than just creating a contract between the licensee and licensor. Licensing is a different way of thinking about what to do with intellectual property - it is a mindset that sees what others don't see; a mindset that recognizes the value of an IP in different ways. For instance, a patented design feature used to streamline an aircraft also works to enhance designs in automobiles. Or a copyrighted rock-and-roll song with lyrics and rhythms works well for a television ad.

Licensing lets other people market and sell the products, services, or technologies created from your intellectual property. It brings together the IP owner with the marketers, companies, and entrepreneurs with the ability in manufacturing, distribution, marketing, and sales. In some cases, it's a single manufacturer who generates a single source of income. In other cases, it's several companies producing multiple income sources. For instance, at the core of an entertainment property is a TV show or a movie. From there, it's licensed into many product categories: toys, T-shirts, beverages, etc. Each of those categories then generates revenue back to the entertainment property (the TV show or movie).

Developing an intellectual property is another way of using licensing. If you don't have the financial resources, you can partner with a company to complete the development and test marketing. Many industries use this strategy, such as pharmaceuticals, biotech, and healthcare technology, which requires long testing cycles and regulatory approvals before a new product gets into the consumer market.

Many excellent and innovative products, services, and technologies are sitting unused because IP owners don't know how to collaborate with licensing partners. And that's what the licensing process is: identifying and contracting with the companies and professionals who have the resources and ability to get your IP into the commercial market.

Licensing works together with marketing. It's part of the marketing strategy, or should be, because it's a low-risk, low-cost approach for launching new innovative products and services. The more you understand about sound marketing principles, the faster you'll make a fortune in licensing. A successful licensing program builds on a marketing basics foundation: who is the customer, why would they buy what you're offering, how much will they pay, and how do you reach them?

Licensing creates multiple sources of income from IP. It generates new streams of money for both the IP owner and the licensees. IP rights are licensed to many users' simultaneously in different ways and for various purposes, such as in different countries, for varying lengths of time, for different products and industries, and different amounts of royalty payments.

Why Licensing?

For people who like to invent, licensing is a great way to free you up to do what you do best: develop and create. I speak with many inventors who've created lots of incredible new IPs but don't know how to make money with them. If you're one of these inventors, licensing is the best route for you. If you're a business owner, licensing allows you tap into this ocean of inventors with market-ready intellectual property. It's one of the fastest and lowest-cost ways to "develop" new products or services.

And the best thing about licensing is it's very lucrative. Globally, licensing generates billions of dollars every year. It generates income for the creative people who create the IP - the inventors of the products and services. It's lucrative for the licensing agents and other third parties who spot new opportunities and trends for IP. It generates new revenues for the companies who license and bring the products and services to market.

And finally, licensing trickles down the line to the contract manufacturers, designers, distributors, and all the other companies whose business activities support developing, producing, and selling the intellectual property around the world.

The Language of Licensing

Before continuing here's a quick review of the language of licensing - some basic vocabulary used in the world of licensing.

IP - This is the abbreviation for intellectual property. In this book, it refers to all types of IP, including patents, trademarks, copyrights, and trade secrets.

Licensor - This is the IP owner, who is an inventor or company that owns the IP.

Licensee - This is the IP renter, usually a company who is licensing the rights to the IP.

Royalty – This is the term describing payments between the licensor and licensee.

License or License Agreement – A written agreement between a licensee and licensor that details what's licensed, how it's used, who does what and when, and how the deal ends.

While there is much more to the language of licensing, these are the most common licensing expressions I refer to in this book.

CHAPTER 2

The Five Golden Rules of Licensing

The goal of licensing is to transform IP into income-producing products, services, and technologies. Just like other types of income-producing assets, such as buying and selling real estate, it requires understanding an essential set of rules to succeed. Licensing is no different. Let's start with the five golden rules of licensing.

1. Companies Don't License IP; They License Money

The first rule is to talk about money, not your IP. The more you can show a licensing partner why your IP is valuable to them, the more interested they will be in licensing it.

Remember, the number one key issue for a potential licensing partner is the value of your IP. If it doesn't work, it's not valuable. The real value of your IP is the way a licensing partner can use it to generate revenues, cut costs, increase profit margins, or gain a competitive advantage. A licensee must feel your IP is worth the risk they are taking to bring it to the market. You've got to show licensees your IP works, and that customers will buy it.

The more money it can make (or the more significant problem it solves), the more valuable the IP is to them.

Sometimes IP value builds fast, while in other cases it takes time. No matter what kind of IP you own, there are specific actions you must take to establish its value. If you don't do something to prove your IP is valuable, then nobody will want to license it. In other words, to successfully license your IP, you must determine its marketability. Marketability is what you're doing when you take steps to confirm, prove, test, and generate some level of customer feedback and sales from your IP. Through this process, you get the information to help you determine the money-making potential of your IP (see Rule #3).

2. Find the Right Partner

The second rule is to look for the right kind of licensing partner. Don't jump at the first offer that comes along. The right partner is not necessarily the one offering the most money. In many cases, that kind of partner will only get you a "quick in and out" of the market.

Remember, there is a life cycle for everything. The right partner is the one who can nurture your IP, build your licensing program, and create long-term cash flow, not the one who promises a lot of money up front. Ultimately, if your IP has long-term potential, small gains can result in the most profitable licensing deal.

Do your homework and make sure this potential partner has the money, people, and right resources to bring your IP into the market. Getting the right partner ensures your best chance of market success.

3. Numbers, Numbers, Numbers

The third rule is "Know the numbers" - the cost to produce and deliver, and the price and the profit margins. The better you understand how profitable your IP is, the stronger the position you will be in to license it. It's one of the first questions a licensing partner will ask.

If figuring out the numbers is not your strength, find somebody to help you. Enlist the aid of an accountant, or someone experienced with similar products or services who will understand how to create the revenue model for your intellectual property.

4. Be Prepared

Rule number four is preparation, preparation, preparation. All the things done through the licensing process – from marketing your IP to meeting potential partners - come down to one thing: the negotiation. You collect information that helps you make intelligent decisions about the business terms and conditions of your license agreement.

Be clear about what you expect and what you need to make a license worthwhile. If the partner cannot give what you need to make the deal work, no matter how harmonious your visions, no matter how well you seem able to get along, then your agreement will fail.

5. You Have One Shot

Rule number five is that you only have one chance to make the right impression. One of the most critical steps in the licensing process is the presentation. Be passionate, exciting, and focused. Licensees will get excited when they see you excited about your IP.

Be concise and tell the right kind of story. Be prepared with your numbers. Be ready to prove how your IP makes money. Know who the right licensing candidates are and deliver your presentation with confidence. Remember, it's a "Show Me the Money" presentation that dramatically increases the odds of convincing a licensee that your IP is worth the risk to license.

A Career in Licensing

How did I get into licensing? Like so many things in life, it just happened. I found an opportunity to join a large studio in the late 1980s.

Licensing was not a big business for the studios in those days. There weren't many people who even had experience in licensing. When I started, I knew very little about licensing. The studio was producing a movie based on a comic book character that hadn't been in the public eye for over 20 years. My first assignment was to find companies willing to get a license to make and sell products based on the movie characters.

At first, it was slow going. Many large companies didn't think the movie would sell. It was the smaller entrepreneurial companies that were willing to take the risk. Shortly after the studio started promoting the film, it suddenly caught consumers attention and quickly turned into a hundred-million-dollar licensing franchise.

The studio's licensing business quickly grew, and soon I was licensing cartoon TV shows, movies, live action sitcoms and even a joint venture license between the studio and a professional sports league. I worked with companies big and small, learning creative ways of structuring licensing agreements. Each deal was different; I negotiated contracts with many companies, licensing rights for hundreds of products and promotional partner tie-ins that are part and parcel of big movie projects.

After spending over a decade on the studio side of licensing and learning the licensing business, it was time to set up my shop. I've now represented many clients in licensing out their IP and acquiring a variety of licenses, from health care technology to consumer brands to entertainment-based IP.

Part of my most significant value to my clients is my expertise on how to market the IP, negotiate the licenses, and structure the royalty payments to keep the upfront costs low, and who the right people to talk to are. Licensing is about relationships. This kind of business development all comes down to having relationship-building skills and the ability to create a rapport.

I've always been an entrepreneur at heart, and one of the reasons I love licensing is that it's very entrepreneurial (provided you're not working in a big licensing division at a major corporation). You never know what the next big IP and licensing opportunity will be, but with so much intellectual property in the world, there's no limit to the wealth-creating possibilities.

Why I Wrote This Book

When I set up my consulting business, I had worked with people who understood licensing. So I assumed everyone did. I quickly discovered that most people didn't know what licensing is and how it works.

To understand licensing, you need to understand what IP is, and I'm talking beyond the standard terms of the patent, trademark, and copyright (which I'll get to in later chapters). To understand IP, you have to step back and look at the creation of most wealth.

All wealth is intangible until some action converts it into tangible wealth. That's what IP is...an intangible wealth asset. But most people don't know how to create wealth with intellectual property. There's a lack of valuable education and training on how to make money with intellectual property. It's not taught in any schools, and there is only limited teaching within the university curriculum.

There are two sides to intellectual property - the legal side and the money side. Most people are familiar with the legal side of IP and know very little about the money-making side of licensing. Licensing is the money-making side. Legal is an integral part of licensing, but the main focus of licensing is an activity (action) that transforms your IP into a tangible money-making form.

I'm often amazed at how few people understand this. They often assume that licensing is a legal thing or a legal process, which makes sense when you consider that the bulk of information about licensing focuses on the legal side. Most articles about licensing talk about the legal issues, most classes on licensing concentrate on the legal side, and licensing is a subject mostly taught at law schools.

The problem is the skills you have learned focus on creating wealth with tangible products (and even services). That's one of the biggest obstacles to making money with intellectual property - lacking an understanding and the right knowledge and licensing skills.

The result is too many people making wrong assumptions, making too many mistakes and completely misunderstanding the basics of what licensing is all about. You wind up starting with a shaky foundation on a long, frustrating, and costly licensing journey. But there's no reason it must continue that way. That's why I wrote this book.

Whether you are an inventor with new IP, a business ready to expand, or an entrepreneur looking for the next big opportunity, this book gives you the real-world information you can use now to start making money with your IP.

The book chapters follow the steps in the licensing process. But understand the process doesn't always move sequentially. If you're licensing a new IP, then you'll most likely follow these steps in order. If your IP is in the market, either as a product, service, or technology, a potential licensing partner might approach you. In this case, you might go right to the chapters on negotiating and licensing agreements. And for most IP owners, you'll do some of these steps simultaneously.

CHAPTER 3

Three Ways to Make Money with IP

There are several ways of making money with intellectual property. Setting up a business to make and sell it yourself is one option. Selling your IP outright is a second option. Licensing it out to other companies is a third way. The question is which one is the best option for you?

To help answer that, here are the pros and cons of the first two as compared to licensing.

Sell the IP

Selling your intellectual property is transferring ownership to another person or company for a set price.

If you sell outright before it's in the marketplace, you don't know if you'll get the fair value for your IP. Once you sell it, there is no going back. There are no refunds in the world of intellectual property. For example, you might sell your patent and get $500 today. But what if the product becomes a hit? You sold the patent for $500 but new patent owner rakes in $500,000 in profits!

When the inventor of one of the most famous boy's action figure sold his patent to the world's largest toy company, they gave him a choice. He could sell it for $100,000 or "license" it for $50,000 upfront plus a one percent royalty once sales exceeded $7 million. He sold it for $100,000 and lost out on an estimated $20 million in royalties over the next 30 years.

Keep in mind that most IP is hard to sell. Many studies confirm that most issued patents aren't worth anything. Unless it's tested in the market with sales or a running business around it, selling it is difficult. If you do find a buyer, most likely they will offer a much smaller price than what you think it is worth. The buyer won't pay much for an IP that hasn't generated any money. Without any sales, you'll be hard pressed to justify your asking price.

Or you could license it out, and receive royalties. Three or four years out, it becomes very successful, and suddenly your IP is worth hundreds of thousands if not millions. Along the way, you increase its value and ultimately to sell it at a higher price.

One of my clients invented a new accessory item for the professional hair care salon market, and a company contacted him about licensing it. As part of the deal, the company wanted to buy out the IP at some point in the licensing agreement. Plus they were also willing to pay a royalty after the acquisition for five years.

The buyout terms required the company reaching certain minimum royalty payment milestones over the first five years of the agreement. If they met or exceeded those, they had the option right to purchase the IP at a price calculated using an average royalty paid formula.

Make It Yourself

Starting your business around your IP takes time, money, and resources. You must also get (i.e., hire) the necessary experience, whether it's marketing, sales, distribution, or production.

In today's global innovation economy, the lifespan of technologies is shrinking. Most patents outlive the economic life of the product or technology. Some studies report the average lifespan of new technologies is 18-24 months. That doesn't leave much time for your startup to get established in the marketplace.

Keep in mind that the odds of succeeding as a startup are low. Statistically, most startups fail within five years. If you go this route and run out of money, it's tough to switch to another option.

Before starting a business around your IP, consider your tolerance of risk, and whether you can successfully manage the uncertainties, delays and other unknown issues that pop-up. If your IP is in an industry dominated by large companies, is capital-intensive to develop and build, requires regulatory approval, or will be technologically obsolete in just a few years, licensing is a far better option than starting a business.

Licensing

Your third option is to license your IP in return for a royalty. For most IP owners, this is an easier and less risky option than to make and sell it directly. It's an ideal option if you lack the resources to get your IP into the market, or you're not interested in starting and running a company. Licensing a well-established company already making and selling products similar to your IP also increases your chances for success in the market.

Licensing requires no upfront cost, and it minimizes your downside risk. It lets you control your IP rights. You rent out (i.e., license out) the rights to make, use, and sell it to other companies. Licensing is a faster way to get your intellectual property to market - months vs. the average two years it takes to start and grow a new business.

Licensing is flexible and lets you create multiple income opportunities with your IP. You can divide rights geographically or by distribution channel. A good example is a popular kid's book. It has an almost boundless number of licensing options ranging from books, movies, video games, theme parks, cartoons, toys, clothing, and so on.

If you want to sell direct, you can also keep some or all the rights for specific markets or product formats.

Summary of Key Points

So how do you decide which option to use and when? My recommendation is to start with licensing. It decreases your risk and increases the chance for commercial success. It's a faster track to the marketplace, let's you tap into companies who already have the wheel in motion, and is a less risky way to make money with your IP.

By the way, licensing isn't mutually exclusive, and can be combined with the other two. Licensing a larger partner is often the first step toward a buyout. As they use your IP, it generates revenues, builds value, and leads to a higher buyout price.

If you're a startup, you can use licensing to generate new revenues in other markets while you focus on building your core market. If you're an inventor and don't want to run a company, you'll avoid the time and unknown risks of starting a new business.

CHAPTER 4

The Deed to Your Property

Intellectual property is similar to real estate. When you buy real estate, you get a deed to the property with rights to use it, develop it, and sell it. These rights are bundled up in the form of a house or building. And it also may include other rights such as mineral, water, and easement rights.

When you register your IP, it's a deed to your property. It protects your rights to make, use, and sell it. Your idea becomes an intellectual property when you protect the legal rights to it. Protecting your IP prevents others from trading on your hard work and allows you to capture the return on your investment.

If you don't protect it you face some risks including loss of income if someone uses your IP without paying royalties, someone walks off with your trade secrets and gives them to your competitor, or you get a letter threatening litigation from a company claiming you are infringing on their IP.

One of the world's best-known technology companies made this fatal mistake when they failed to patent their user mouse and graphic user interface. The result was nimble competitors who capitalized on this deadly mistake and quickly generated tens of millions of dollars using their innovation.

Two Ways to Protect IP Rights

Almost anything can be licensed as long as it contains rights that can be protected. There are two ways to protect intellectual property rights:

- By registering with a government agency and;

- By maintaining the secrecy or confidentiality of information.

Registered IP includes patents, copyrights, and trademarks. The electronics, drug companies, and other high tech industries typically protect their products with patents. Well-known brands use registered trademarks, and movie and TV shows are most often registered copyrights.

Unregistered IP is known as trade secrets. It includes know-how, business process, formulas, recipes, and other confidential information - anything you've created that helps you make a profit and don't want anyone to know how you do it. Trade secrets such as the formula for major soda brands and the algorithms for the big search engine brands are examples of unregistered IP.

It's not uncommon for both types of IP rights to exist in one product, such as trademark for a soda brand combined with trade secret formula.

Here's a quick review of each type of IP and how it's protected.

Patents

You can file patents several ways – directly as the inventor or through patent agents and patent attorneys. Patent rights only prohibit others from using the parts of your IP included in the patent claims. If you improve the way smartphones function, those functions are the claims in your patent, and your rights only cover those enhanced functions, not the entire smartphone.

There are several types of patents. The most common are utility and design patents. A design patent protects the way that an article looks, and used in industries where the product's aesthetic qualities are of particular significance, such as clothing, furniture, beverage containers, smartphones, and even computer icons. Functional inventions, such as a new type of vehicle, are utility patents. It can also cover the functional feature of clothing or accessories such as a jacket with an improved insulation system.

Your patent can also include an unregistered part, such as know-how about the manufacturing process, a specific way to design it or some other method that makes it faster, cheaper, or better. For example, a build-to-order production model that slashes the cost of delivering the patented product to customers.

Don't overlook this unregistered part of your patent when negotiating your licensing agreement. If it's applied to other products or industries, you can license it with or without your patent.

A Quick Word about Provisional Patents

It is not a patent. It's a document that holds your place in line and gives you 12 months to file a full patent application. It's useful if you're still developing and testing the technology or product, and you need to show information about it to potential investors.

It gives you time to figure out whether your technology is practical and worth getting a full patent. But it's not very useful, in my opinion, for licensing. It doesn't offer a potential licensing partner any value because the technology or product is still a significant risk since its commercial viability is unknown. In my experience, most companies, especially the larger ones, are not interested in licensing a provisional patent.

If you do decide to file a provisional patent, work with a qualified patent attorney or agent to get it done correctly. With changes in the patent filing laws (the U.S. is now the first-to-file system); it requires more than just filling out the application. If you don't do it correctly, it can come back to haunt you down the road when you file to get a non-provisional patent.

Trademarks

You launched a new product into the gift market. But you never bothered to make sure your trademark is available for that category. A competitive product shows up using the same mark, and worse, you get a "cease and desist" letter saying you're infringing on their trademark.

Registering a trademark is done by specific product or service categories. Just because you register in one category doesn't mean someone else can't register and use it for another. That's why it's essential to run a trademark search before using it.

Trademarks come in many different formats. The most common forms are words (bubble wrap), names (such as your product or company or even your name), and symbols (think fruit, icons or multiple letters), or some combination (your company name with a symbol). There are also other types of non-conventional trademarks, including color, scent, and, sound.

A trademark is used to distinguish or identify the source of goods. Service marks are like trademarks except that they apply to services rather than products. The same word or symbol can be both a trademark and a service mark. For example, a restaurant logo is a service mark for food services, and as a trademark for products such as desserts, sauces, and beverages.

Registering a trademark protects it, and, in some countries, also through using it. You can register trademarks at the state and federal level. State registration only provides limited protection to a particular geographic area. To truly protect your product and brand, registering your trademark with the U.S. Patent and Trademark Office is by far the smartest option.

Good examples are the kid's properties I licensed while at the studios. The studios trademarked these properties around the world, in dozens of different product and service categories. But these were more than just a single character or brand name. Many of these entertainment properties included lots of characters, vehicles, and "cool" fighting accessories which, in many cases, were also trademarked (these are known as "sub-brands"). The more these characters were seen on TV and in movies, the more valuable the trademarks became (and the more money they generated in royalty revenues). Registering, tracking, and stopping infringer's kept the legal department very busy.

Trademarks, unlike patents and copyrights, are low maintenance and relatively low-cost. Your trademark can last indefinitely, as long as you're current with all the registration requirements.

Copyrights

Copyrights protect ideas expressed in different tangible formats. These include movies, TV shows, books, paintings, sculptures, artwork, photography, music, and more. It also includes other "non-artistic" forms such as computer programs, product label designs, and architectural works. Anything that is created and performed or put down on paper or film is copyright.

A copyright gives you the sole right to publish (i.e., copy or broadcast) or perform (adaptations) your copyrighted work. It also prohibits what is known as derivatives without your permission.

It is not necessary to register your work to get a copyright. But if you don't register your copyright, you'll be unable to enforce your rights through the courts. And that's just what happened to one of my clients. Her late husband was a photographer who took thousands of pictures of Marilyn Monroe in her early years. It was a vast collection, and she didn't keep tight control of it. We discovered a company using some of the photos and selling limited edition reprints. My client filed an infringement lawsuit. Even though it was a case of infringement, she was not able to enforce legal action in court because she hadn't registered the photos for copyright protection.

Registering your copyright is some of the cheapest IP insurance you can buy. At the very least, it protects your rights, and you'll have the legal teeth at your disposal to action against the infringer.

Trade Secrets

The term "trade secret" refers to information and knowledge that is kept confidential, and it's valuable. It's valuable because it is something that you have or do that no one else can do.

Types of trade secret IP include business processes, customer lists, survey results, computer algorithms, formulas, product designs, websites, software source codes, and more. Some examples of well-known trade secrets include soda formulas, recipes for fried chicken, and search engine algorithms.

23

Trade secret licenses, unlike patents, can last forever. Even if a trade secret later becomes public, royalty payments under trade secret licensing agreements can continue indefinitely. A classic example is the Listerine mouthwash formula. In 1881, Dr. J.J. Lawrence licensed the formula with no time limit. Although it became public, the original licensing agreement continued to generate royalties.

You don't register trade secrets with a government agency to protect it; you keep the information confidential. Trade secret protection lasts for as long as the secret is kept confidential. Once it becomes public information, trade secret protection ends.

Make sure you're taking steps to protect your trade secrets. If you're a business owner, set up internal and external controls (i.e., who gets access and a tracking process) to protect its confidentiality. Get signed work-for-hire agreements from employees or independent contractors creating anything for your business or developing your IP. Be sure it details you or your company owns all the work created by them.

International Registration

Countries around the world now recognize that intellectual property as critical to their growth and prosperity. IP laws are quickly harmonizing around the world, as most countries have enacted laws to protect the primary forms of IP (patents, trademarks, industrial designs, and copyright).

While intellectual property laws vary from country to country, the registration process for patents, trademarks, and copyrights are similar. Several agreements between the U.S. and other countries enable the concurrent registration of patents and trademarks in multiple countries with one set of documents. Rather than filing applications in each country, you can file a single application, in one language, and pay one application fee to register your IP in many different countries. It reduces your time and costs to obtain international protection, and in the case of patents, gives you time to test the commercial viability of your invention. For example, filing one international patent application (also known as a PCT application which is short for the *Patent Cooperation Treaty*) lets you apply for protection of an invention in over one hundred countries worldwide.

You can do the same thing with copyrights. The U.S. has registration relationships with many countries around the world that provides for automatic recognition of copyright works of authors. You get the same copyright protection status as a resident, meaning if someone copies your book without your permission in France, you can sue under French copyright law.

You can file a trademark for all countries in the European Union simultaneously instead of registering country by country. In most countries, trademark registration is mandatory, and many countries require local use of the registered mark to keep up the registration. If you're going international, be sure to research your trademark in each market. Check with the trademark office in each country to make sure (1) your mark is available and (2) you understand the registration requirements.

Before registering an IP in any county, seek out the advice of a qualified legal expert who is familiar with foreign intellectual property laws. They can guide and help you avoid the pitfalls of foreign IP registration.

Summary of Key Points

Just as real and personal property rights protect your ownership interest in tangible assets like real estate and automobiles, IP rights protect your ownership interest in intellectual property - such as the idea behind an invention, the music score for a Broadway play, or the name or logo used to brand a product.

Be careful not to get bogged down in the legal protection process. Rather than trying to protect everything, focus on the most valuable and commercially viable parts of your IP. For instance, if you have multiple inventions, don't patent all of them. Instead, focus on the one that has the most commercial opportunity. That's the one to protect and license.

You can also protect your IP using combinations of patents, trademarks, copyrights, and trade secrets. For example, software copyright, a trademarked product name, and the source code is a trade secret. It provides multiple layers of protection and extends the time the protection is available.

Once you protect it, you have to safeguard it, use it, and if necessary, prevent others from using it illegally.

CHAPTER 5

Show Me the Money

When I began my career at the studios, the first property I licensed was a movie based on a comic book character not seen by the public in over 20 years. The challenge was nobody thought the IP would make any money. Not one major toy company wanted to license it. The retailers didn't think it would sell. And the studio feared the movie would flop in theaters. The only companies interested in taking a shot were startups and small companies willing to take the risk on an "unknown" entertainment IP. When the movie released, it quickly became a merchandising juggernaut, generating hundreds of millions of dollars in retail sales. And suddenly, every major consumer products company wanted to license it.

The Number 1 Rule of Licensing

The Number 1 rule of licensing: licensees don't license IP, they license MONEY. Understand that "licensees buy 'MONEY' - NOT patents, trademarks, and copyrights."

Creating value is the secret to attracting licensing partners. Proving the IP works – solves a problem, lowers costs, increases revenues, or meets a need and customers will pay for it - is essential. IP value derives from what your IP does. It's the economic benefits (i.e., money) your IP delivers.

Four Ways an IP is Valuable to a Licensing Partner

Generating revenues is the number one reason most companies license IP. But it's not the only reason. Lowering costs, creating new products, and improving products are the other reasons companies license IP. The more of these your IP offers, the higher its value and the price (royalty) a licensing partner is willing to pay for it.

1. It Helps Them Increase Revenues from Their Existing Products (or Services)

When I was licensing the popular kid's movies at the studios, the licensee's product sales skyrocketed when these entertainment brands took off. Many of these companies had their own "brands," but they also recognized the sales power of licensing rights to a popular kid's movie or TV show.

A well-known brand or big movie franchise is a valuable IP because applying it to your existing products can increase your revenues. The price paid (i.e., royalty rate) to license these properties can run 10–15% or more.

2. It Reduces Costs or Increases Profits on Existing Sales

One of my clients was a new toy company who wanted to enter the US toy market. Trying to build a new toy brand in the US is a costly proposition. Instead, we licensed several well-known kids TV shows that had big licensing programs with lots of licensed products at retail.

These brands gave the company immediate access to those retailers. By using this strategy, the toy company was able to get into the US market much faster and at a fraction of the cost of building their brand. They paid a royalty of 8-10% to the brand owner but saved millions in promotional dollars (and got their products into the retail market much faster).

Lower promotional costs are just one way IP reduces costs. Another of my clients' created a workplace safety training process for big manufacturing companies that reduce injuries and saves medical insurance costs. A third example is an automated manufacturing process that saves the licensee 50% of their manufacturing costs.

3. It Creates a Product Category or Industry

A breakthrough intellectual property is something completely new - a disruptive technology that creates not only a new market or industry but in turn leads to the creation of other IPs. Some of history's most prominent breakthrough technologies include the printing press (1450), steam engine (1712), telephone (1876) and the automobile (1878).

In the 20th century, technology such as the computer and Internet created hundreds of new industries, which in turn spawned millions of new intellectual properties around the world and hundreds of millions of dollars in licensing revenues.

But a disruptive technology doesn't always need to be something completely new. The smartphone created a new market for Internet access and is displacing laptops as the mainstream choice for users going online.

Disruptive IP royalty rates range from 7% - 15% and depend on what's required to create and build the market or industry for the IP.

4. It Improves a Product or Technology

Intellectual property is valuable if it improves quality, reliability, ease of use, lowers costs, or opens new market applications. Incremental IP (such as a chip inside a computer) is another type of IP that helps increase revenue by improving a product by making it better, faster, or cheaper. It's ideal for licensing because it's less risky than breakthrough IP with unknown markets.

I'm always amazed at the creativity of inventors when it comes to this type of IP. One of my clients invented an improvement to the toilet. It's an access panel to quickly clear clogs without the need of plungers and expensive plumbers. It also reduces downtime for many businesses, especially hotels and restaurants, where clogged toilets often result in lost revenues.

Even a small improvement can have significant commercial value, especially in highly competitive markets. The wireless industry is one example. There are thousands of patents to enhance consumer use and experience with smart-phones and other wireless devices. Many of these patents are incremental types of IP, such as LED screens, app software, keyboard designs, and a host of electronic components that are necessary for all wireless devices to work.

How much a licensee will pay ultimately depends on how big a part your IP plays in extending or improving their product or technology.

6 Ways to Prove IP Value

The best thing you can do to succeed in licensing is to prove your technology or product works and customers will buy it. Instead of spending all your time trying to build a business, set up distribution channels, or hire people, use that money to develop and market test your technology or product. The better you can document this - the more you can prove its value in the market - the higher the likelihood you'll succeed in licensing.

Proving you IP is valuable is more than just obtaining a patent, copyright or trademark. You need honest, unbiased feedback. If your invention is new, is it better? Is it different? Your friends are not the best way to get honest feedback. They will likely say only positive things to avoid conflict or to show their support.

So how do you confirm your intellectual property is better, and customers love it? Here are six of the best ways:

1. Selling

Selling is one of your best ways of getting feedback and proving customer demand. You don't have to sell a lot of your product or technology to validate its market value. One of my clients built some early versions of their product and sold about 2000 units. Because they received a great response in the form of testimonials (and sales), it was enough to validate their technology. Plus they backed that up with lots of technology research. When I presented it to potential licensing partners, ultimately we were successful in signing one because the technology was validated and they saw the value in it.

2. Social Media

One of the fastest ways is testing it on social media outlets, such as Facebook, LinkedIn, and Twitter. These can play a big part in your licensing initiatives. You can create an ongoing dialog with and get feedback from customers or product innovators. Tweeting test results or live updates from a trade show is another example.

3. Create IP Awareness

The third way is to build awareness about your IP. For a brand, movie, or TV show, awareness is what creates the value. The more awareness there is about it, the higher its value. If you created an idea for a new kid's character, the best way to create value is to get in front of kids. You can put it on the website, show it on social media sites, publish a book, or even develop a quick animation video. The same is true for products and technologies. Whatever you do to build awareness about your IP translates into value for a potential licensing partner.

A massive fan base or potential customer following can make your IP much more appealing to a potential licensee. In one case, I helped a client license their non-profit characters to a large school product supplier. Their characters educated kids about obesity, and they promoted them at special events to help kids stay fit. They used their website and social media to build a fan base of tens of thousands of school kids.

4. Crowd Sourcing

Crowdsourcing helps speed up the process for both new product ideas and early customer feedback. Rather than guessing what your customer wants, you can use crowdsourcing to find out if what you invented is what customers actually will want and buy. Crowdsourcing reduces product development risk at the concept stage. It also gives you new ideas for your product that you wouldn't think of on your own. Some sites for crowdsourcing customer feedback include suggestionbox.com or Feedbackify.com.

One thing to keep in mind is your sharing your intellectual property with lots of people. That leaves you open to the risk of someone else using it. Before sharing your IP on a crowdsourcing platform, make sure you confirm that all information is confidential and that you will own the all the crowdsourced work.

5. Talk to a Retail Buyer

If your intellectual property is a new product that will be sold through retail, talking to a buyer's one of the best things you can do. If a buyer likes it and will buy it that means there's a lot of value for your licensing partner. And I can tell you, nothing attracts a licensing partner better than an interested retail buyer, especially from a major department or mass-market store. Trade shows are an excellent way to meet retail buyers. You can also get direct buyer feedback for new product inventions at websites such as buyerly.com.

6. Sample It

If your IP is still in development, or you are just getting started, then sampling is one of the best ways to prove its value. You can do test marketing and give away your products or services to get customer feedback, testimonials, and proof of your IP's market potential. If your IP is a tangible product, such as a new invention, then consider giving away samples at events. If it's intangible such as software, let customers experience it or use it in some manner. I had a client who invented a biodegradable material for making umbrellas. They would produce samples and give them away at outdoor events, green events, and especially at rainy day events. Customers loved the umbrellas, and they wound up attracting several umbrella manufacturers interested in licensing their IP.

Licensing partners like IP that has customers ready to buy. Nothing sells a license better than customers who want to buy your products, services, or technology. Think about what you can do with your IP to get it in your customer's hands. Get their testimonials and let your customers help you transform your IP into money making licensing deals.

Summary of Key Points

The most important thing you must do to move your idea from a concept into a "licensable" intellectual property is to prove it makes money and is worth the "risk." Remember, registering a copyright or trademark, or receiving a patent grant doesn't mean the IP is worth anything. Unless it works - increases revenues or lowers costs, provides a competitive advantage or does something cheaper, faster and better, and customers will buy it - it isn't worth anything.

Value is what licensing partners are willing to pay for in royalties. New market-ready technology for a multi-billion dollar industry is valuable. On the other hand, an untested new product has little value.

Some things you can do to prove IP value include test marketing, selling, testing online by making offers through social media, or using a "crowd-source" testing service. Customer feedback is one of the most potent ways of confirming IP value.

Finally, the best agreements are ones that involve licensing your IP at an appropriate stage of development. If you sign a license too early, you wind up getting a lower royalty than if you had taken another couple of months to confirm your IP value. On the other hand, many licensees regret deals for IP too early in the game, having saddled themselves with excessive development and testing work that costs them time, money, and anxiety.

Remember, licensing partners DON'T license IP – they license money. The more you show a licensing partner why your IP is valuable to them, the more interested they will be in licensing it.

market opportunity + Data

CHAPTER 6

Getting Ready to Get it Right

One of the first questions I ask IP owners who have tried to license their intellectual property is "what information are you providing about your IP"? Most often, it's a lengthy document with lots of technical jargon, market facts and figures, and the complete history of how they developed it.

If you are unsuccessful in licensing, it may be a timing issue, but, more than likely, it's a lack of the right information and a poor presentation that did you in.

To succeed in licensing requires providing the right information in the right order and the right way to make it happen. The trick is to get all these rights done in the right way. If you're not ready and you don't have a game plan, you'll wind up unprepared to answer questions, provide information, or worse, lose track of what information you sent to whom.

The starting point to successfully delivering the right information in the right way in developing the four core tools necessary to provide potential licensing partners the type of information they need to make a decision.

The Introduction Email

When first contacting a potential partner, the essential tool is a very concise introduction email about your IP - what it is and how it solves a big problem.

- Will it increase their revenues?

- Does it lower their costs?

- Is it a breakthrough technology that will revolutionize their industry?

Whatever it is, that is what you must hit them within your first communication. The goal is to find out 1) if the company is interested in your IP and 2) confirm who to speak with about licensing. To carry out that goal, here are some tips for creating your introduction email.

Keep your introduction email short and to the point. The right introduction email lets the reader quickly figure out if it's something they're interested in pursuing. Ideally, it's less than 100 words and summarizes your IP in one or two sentences explaining what problem it solves or pain it relieves. Don't ramble about the history, background, or potential.

Here's one example I have used with great success.

Would you be interested in licensing a patented blue light toothbrush technology clinically proven to whiten teeth 25% faster and improve gum health in as little as two weeks?

This opening sentence summarizes the IP and what problem it solves. It tells the reader what the IP is (patented toothbrush technology), who it's for (consumers), what it does (whiten teeth and improve gum health) and the results it achieves (clinically proven to work within two weeks).

A variation is asking if they are the right person to contact, and if not, who is. It's similar to the first email but with some slight changes.

Here's an example:

Are you the right person to contact about licensing a patented blue light toothbrush technology clinically proven to whiten teeth 25% faster and improve gum health? If you're not the right person to speak with, whom do you suggest I contact?

Here's a fill-in-the-blanks breakdown of this email template:

Are you the right person to contact about an XYZ technology? It's a (market tested, patented, clinically tested, etc.) XYZ that (key problem or pain point solved, e.g., better, faster, cheaper), which (key benefit to end-user or customer, e.g., increases revenues, reduces costs, etc.) by (quantified results such as 50%, 30 million in revenue, etc.).

Nothing puts off a potential partner more than having to wade through a long email or document to try and figure out what the IP does. Remember their priority is running their business, and if you don't make it simple for them to understand your IP and the licensing opportunity, they won't be interested.

Licensing Opportunity One Sheet

The first *non-confidential* information you send to potential licensing partners after they respond to your introduction email. The best format is for this is a one or two-page summary highlighting the IP and the licensing opportunity (you can also provide this information in a follow-up email).

The key word is "concise." Think of it as a resume. Potential partners don't and won't take the time to read the entire history of your IP. Here's an example template for developing your one sheet.

- Background - What's the big problem your IP solves (such as addresses obesity problem by lowering fat content in fried foods).

- Milestones - What is the IP status (such as the stage of development, working prototypes, or selling in the marketplace)?

- History - A BRIEF history of the IP, such as its development, and protection status.

- IP Details - What it is, how it works, and why it's better (do not include confidential information such as trade secrets), with a few key statistics of supporting research data if available.

- Customers - Who are the customers, and why will they buy the product/service/technology.

- Licensing – Some general information about licensing IP rights such as exclusivity, territories, etc.

Make sure it looks professional and includes the correct contact information such as your name, telephone, email address, and website.

The Licensing Information Package

A well-documented licensing package speeds the process by shortening the time it takes a licensee to complete their evaluation of your IP. It includes more non-confidential information about your IP - patents granted (and applications), trademark registrations, test markets, product sales, customer feedback, and other supporting information. Provide the licensing package only after a potential partner confirms they're interested.

If you have many forms of information, such as videos, audio presentations or lengthy documents, it's better to offer it from a cloud storage system (such as Google or Dropbox) and provide links where a potential partner can view and download the information. It's the best and easiest way to offer your IP information. It's also the best way to control and track your information by using passwords (if necessary) to grant access to or download the information.

"Available for Licensing" Website

We live in an Internet-connected world, and there is no better showcase for your IP than on your website. It's one of the first places potential licensing partners will go to find information quickly about the IP. And it's also a way to get qualified leads that can ultimately lead to a licensing deal.

Design your web site with the audience in mind, meaning the licensee. Include all the *non-confidential* information about your intellectual property on the website. For example, if you invented a new toy, the audience would be toy manufacturers. Provide all the information a toy company would be interested in knowing, such as how the toy works (such as videos or animation), who the target market is (boys, girls, etc.), the status of any testing or sales, and what rights are available for licensing (this will also be in your licensing package).

One of my clients developed a frequency technology used for treating a variety of medical issues - from trauma to pre/post-surgery recovery. They created a website to show how the technology works, the science behind it, and a library of the research studies. It was updated with results from new research reports and was a time saver because the research was one of the first things potential licensees wanted to check. Rather than going back and forth sending documents, I referred them to the website.

You can do the same thing. Post all the information about your IP on your website, so it's easy for potential partners to find it. Plus it's a faster way to keep your IP information up to date. Use your blog to connect with interested companies and keep them informed, and create a page on social media sites such as Facebook and Linked In.

Be sure your website also explains who to contact, what forms to fill out, and how the licensing process works. The better informed potential licensing partners are about your IP, the faster you will be able to create money-making licensing deals.

Summary of Key Points

Your IP is unique. To sell your licensing deal, you must give the right information to the right person at the right company.

The goal of the introduction emails is to find out if they're interested and confirm who to speak with about licensing your IP. Keep it short and focus on the problem/solution benefits of your IP. If you don't make it simple for them to understand the value of your IP, they won't be interested.

A short Licensing Opportunity Summary is the following *non-confidential* information you send to potential licensing partners after they respond to your introduction email. Again, keep it short, no more than two pages. Potential partners don't and won't take the time to read the entire history of your IP.

A licensing website speeds up the licensing process. It's one of the first places potential licensing partners will go to find information about your IP. Keep it updated with all timely information about your IP.

And most important is follow-through. When you follow-up, be sure to give all the information your potential partner needs. Package all the information about your IP in a way that makes it easy for a licensing partner to evaluate your IP.

Make sure you keep these four tools in mind when preparing information about your licensing opportunity. Don't make the mistake of pouring your guts out with the life history of your IP. That's not what a potential licensing partner wants to hear. If you tell them the right story, they'll want to know more, but if you give them the wrong information, they'll wind up walking away.

CHAPTER 7

If You Don't Start the Race, You'll Never Finish

The number one goal of creating an intellectual property is to transform it into money-making products, services, or technologies. But the biggest challenge for most intellectual property owners is how to do it. The question is what to do and how to do it. If you're grappling with this issue, you're not alone.

I'm always amazed when I ask IP owners what they are doing with their intellectual property. Most of the time, the answer is nothing. If you don't start the race, you'll never finish.

Several years ago, I met a gentleman in a restaurant. He'd been sitting on new holographic printing technology for trading cards and didn't know what to do with it. I told him I was in the licensing business and asked him if he ever thought about licensing sports teams for his cards. Since he had mentioned he was a soccer fan during our discussion, I suggested he license well-known soccer teams. The lights went on, and after a couple of meetings, he hired me to help him license the rights to European soccer teams for his trading cards.

At that time, soccer was not as popular as it is today, and it was fairly easy to get licenses to some of the top teams. We

43

traveled to Europe to meet with the popular soccer teams in the UK, France, and Germany. Because the technology was new and innovative, and they loved the idea of featuring the best soccer players, we succeeded in signing licensing deals with each of the soccer teams. These licenses also opened the door to distribution opportunities, and he was able to get his trading cards placed in several big retail chains throughout Europe.

That is an example of direct licensing. It's one of several licensing strategies you can use to license your IP. Whether it's direct to several industries or different products, or a single licensing partner, or through a strategic alliance or joint venture - each is a different strategy. In this chapter, I'll cover four of the most common licensing strategies - direct licensing, sub-licensing, joint venture, and strategic alliance - and how to use them.

Direct Licensing

The two most common ways of direct licensing are exclusive and non-exclusive. An exclusive license puts all your IP eggs in one basket, meaning you are relying on one licensee to make money with your IP. In most situations, it's best to license your IP on a non-exclusive basis. That way you can divide the IP rights and license it into other product categories, as broad as anywhere in the world, or narrowly defined down to the country, product category and even a specific niche market. And you'll also have the option to continue using your IP to sell direct.

When I was licensing movie properties, most of the agreements were non-exclusive except for huge deals, such as a multi-million-dollar toy deal. These licenses included many product categories, and the license terms were precise on distribution channels (such as mass market or toy stores), as well as where they couldn't sell (such as closeout stores). And in some cases, there was even limited exclusive deals for the same type of product – plush toys (stuffed animals) - where the exclusivity applied only to specific distribution channels (gift or toy stores).

Direct licensing is an ideal strategy if you lack the resources to get your IP into the market or you're not interested in starting and running a company. It's less risky than producing and selling yourself. Licensing a well-established company already making and selling products similar to your IP also increases your chances for success in the market.

Well-known consumer brands use licensing as a faster and less risky way to expand into new markets and non-competitive products. They avoid losing a lot of time and money due to the high failure rate of new products and instead focus on supporting their licensing partners.

Direct licensing requires managing the licensing program yourself. If you don't have the time or don't want to do it yourself, you can retain the services of a licensing agent to manage it for you (which I discuss in a later chapter).

Sub-licensing

During my early career at the studios, licensing into Central and South America was always a challenge. Direct licensing was not an option because of weak or nonexistent IP laws. Instead, we licensed a large distributor who, in turn, sub-licensed each company in different product categories. It gave the distributor an added financial incentive to watch licensees and take legal action against piracy. While not the best solution, it was (at that time) the only way to for the studio to maintain control of the IP, keep it protected and generate licensing revenues.

Sub-licensing is a good strategy for broad licensing programs in different product categories and territories, such as brands or characters. In addition to generating revenues directly, your main or anchor licensee also receives part of the royalties from sub-licensing agreements. It's a powerful incentive for them to help build the licensing program. The more successful they are, the more they'll attract other companies to sub-license the IP.

Cutting edge and breakthrough technologies developed by Universities and research labs often use sub-licensing. They include sub-licensing as an added incentive for companies (usually startups) to take development and marketing risk. In return, they can market it directly and re-license it (assuming it works) to another company to generate revenues and receive part of the royalties.

Here's a simple example of how it works. You sign a "master" licensing agreement with a partner at a royalty rate of 5%. The deal includes sub-licensing rights, meaning they can license your IP to other partners under the same terms and conditions as your "master" licensing agreement. If they sign a sub-license agreement for an 8% royalty, they keep 3% and pay you the royalty agreed to in your "master" licensing agreement, which is 5%.

If you don't have the internal resources to manage a licensing program, then sub-licensing makes sense. Be careful with sub-licensing. Control is essential. Be sure your master licensing agreement is specific on the terms for a sub-licensee, which is usually the same terms as the master license.

On the other hand, restricting sub-licensing gives you full control over the licensing process. In this case, it's a direct license with the licensees, and you oversee the development, marketing, and sales of your IP.

Strategic Alliance

A strategic alliance is a good strategy for startups and early-stage companies looking to reduce operational costs and accelerate their growth. A strategic alliance offers a great way to build a market for your IP. Partnering with a larger company helps smaller companies validate their IP technology and business model, get access to capital and other resources.

Co-branding is one of the most common types of strategic alliances. A co-brand license is a strategy you can use to raise awareness and generate sales. Licensing rights to co-package with a well-known brand can create instant credibility by leveraging off the brand's name and market presence. Software bundling is a good example. It features your software and brand as part of the bundled software. You then create special offers for your partner's customers and gain traction into the marketplace. NutraSweet with Diet Coke, MSNBC, and IBM with Intel are all examples of strategic alliance co-branding deals.

Another variation of this is sharing IP to reach new customers. I licensed an up and coming comic book publisher the rights to feature their top comic book characters interacting with the TV show characters in a special edition series. This license is an example of a cross-over strategic alliance where one publishers 'characters' appear in one or more stories interacting with another publisher's (or in this case, entertainment studio) character.

Getting access to lower production costs is a third way of using this strategy. In return, your licensing partner(s) get the rights to make and sell your IP in specific markets or distribution channels. I've used this strategy with several clients who didn't have the financial resources to fund large orders from big retail accounts. In one case, we licensed international rights to a large company in Europe. As part of the deal terms, we negotiated rights to buy products at a cost that was lower than what they were paying to produce it directly.

Joint Ventures (JV)

Industries with capital-intensive R&D and testing phases, such as pharmaceuticals and biotech companies, or industries with lots of IP cross-over, such as smart-phones, often use this strategy. It's faster and cheaper than trying to develop their early stage technologies themselves. You share the development costs and the upside from sales of the IP in the marketplace.

The other type of JV is two partners agreeing to combine their IP in a JV license. I licensed out a JV "IP" combining a popular cartoon show with professional baseball players. The first licensing deal I did was with a new trading card company. They produced a trading card series featuring the cartoon characters, drawn by one of the original animators, playing with some of the most popular retired baseball players. It became a big hit at retail, and the first trading card series generated over $30 million in sales.

Licensing multiple strategic alliances or joint ventures based on territories, use, applications, or product types is another variation. You don't have to include all the rights when using these strategies. In some cases, you can restrict rights to applications of use, such as for the business-to-business market, or certain territories, such as Europe or Asia only. It can continue for the life of a license or dissolve after a specific time. Think of the strategic alliance and joint venture as a partnership for resources.

Summary of Key Points

The most important thing you can do with your intellectual property is to take action. If you don't do something with it, nothing will happen. Think of it this way: when you create intellectual property, you enter the innovation business. Innovation is what drives new products and services. But if you don't act, nothing gets done. Your IP will drift away to someone more motivated to take action with it.

The licensing strategy is what you want to do, and your plan is how you will do it (more on this in a later chapter). It details all the different ways to generate royalty revenue with your IP. For example, it can be non-exclusively to several partners or exclusively to one company. Consumer brands, for example, license into multiple non-competing product categories, such as apparel, toys, and gifts. On the other hand, if it's a single patented product, licensing it to only one or two companies is common.

Timing plays a part in which strategy to use and when. Markets, customers, and competition are always changing, so it's essential to think about using more than one approach. In some situations, you start with one plan and move to a different one, such as from direct licensing to sub-licensing. And you might even use two at the same time, such as a direct license and a joint venture.

If your IP has many licensing options, then an important consideration is how many companies to license. Limiting the number of licensees makes it easier to control and manage. On the other hand, a large number of licensees increase revenue opportunities.

CHAPTER 8

An IP in Motion Makes Money

Don't make the mistake of just randomly going out to the market and throwing information about your IP at a bunch of companies. That won't work. Too many times I've met with IP owners doing just that, only to wind up back where they started - nothing to show for their efforts.

In one case, the inventor created a new zipper technology and tried licensing it to companies he thought would be interested in using it on their products. But he wasn't successful because all he was doing was throwing his IP against the "licensing wall," hoping something would stick. He spent years doing the same thing over and over again only to wind up back where he started - a great IP with no money or resources to get it into the market.

Trying to license your IP without a plan of action is like steering a boat without any navigational charts. You start in one direction, don't get anywhere, then suddenly change course, but never get to where you want to go.

It's a common problem, especially with new inventors trying to license their IP. One of my clients, two inventors, did this (before they hired me) only to discover it didn't work. They knew they wanted to license their IP, but didn't have a plan. They sent their IP information to a friend who knew someone at a company they thought might be interested. Months went by with no response. Now they were stuck trying to figure out what to do next.

The licensing action plan details the different ways or tactics you'll use to move from point A to B. For example, you may decide as a strategy to license your new toy invention in the U.S. to one of the larger toy companies. Your plan identifies which companies are best suited (I cover this in the next chapter) and what you'll do to promote and sell your licensing opportunity to them.

You do this by reaching out through email, providing information, posting news releases, using video presentations, and publicizing your IP in social media channels.

How to Do an Email Campaign

Don't send out your email introduction using a shotgun approach. I suggest sending only one email per contact at each prospect company per week. If you blast your email to six or eight people at the same company, it looks like spam. It's also not professional and more than likely you won't get any response.

If you don't hear back after a couple of weeks, send another follow-up email to confirm if they received your introduction. If you don't receive a response, they are likely not interested (right now) or not the right contact, so move to the next person in the company on your list. But it's not uncommon to get response months after you send the email. I sometimes receive responses six months or more after I sent it.

Keep track of all the emails you send. You can use a spreadsheet to do this, or a better way is using an online CRM system. There are some free and paid systems, such as Hub Spot,

Agile, and others, that make it easy to manage your contacts. Record who you emailed, when you contacted them and whether you received a response.

Make sure you follow-up with everyone who responds. Keep refining your emails to tell a better story and get their attention. Tailor your messages to the company when you get a chance. For example, if you come across an article discussing something relevant to the solution your IP offers, be sure to note that in your email.

Remember to keep your emails short and to the point (I covered this in an earlier chapter). Focus on your best prospects first, and make sure you give them time to respond.

How to Use PR to Promote Your Licensing Opportunity

It's not always the best IP that gets the most licensees...it's the best promoted. A big part of finding licensees is getting the word out about your IP. You have to reach out if you want to connect with licensing partners.

One of the fastest ways to get the word out is through online PR distribution sites. It's an easy tactic you can start using now. Let me share an example from the entertainment industry of what PR can do for your IP. Kid's entertainment properties are very competitive, and no one knows what will be a hit. In one case, a competitive kids TV show was up against the top kid's show I was licensing. They continuously released "news" about the show - when it was launching, what it was about, new licensees signed... anything that was happening with that property. They placed it in trade and licensing magazines and created a licensing buzz. Because manufacturers continually heard about the property, they got a lot of interest, and the PR helped to sign dozens of licensees.

You can do the same thing. There are many free and low-cost PR services you can use to distribute your IP news releases. Most of the sites offer templates to create your PR release. Just follow the template and plug in your information. A couple of the best free sites are PR.com and PRurgent.com. Create a series of updates and announcements about your IP and distribute them weekly. Be sure to include a link to a licensing-specific landing page on your website featuring photos, descriptions, and video of your IP.

Remember, the trick is to communicate continuously with your potential licensing partners. You're creating a discussion. Send out your IP licensing information in small intriguing pieces and give potential partners a reason to contact you. The more you keep the PR dialog going, the more likely it is you'll attract a licensing partner.

A Video is Worth a Million Words

Most companies have a lot on their plates and don't have the time to read all the information they get. And you don't have the time to meet with every potential licensing partner in person.

Creating a video is one of the best and most efficient tools to present your licensing opportunity. You can produce these video yourself for no cost using your computer, some video software and a video camera. A video lets you show an IP in both visual and audio format, whether that is a product, software, video game or movie, and demonstrate how it works or looks. Or if your IP is still in development, you can show pictures, diagrams, or animation and discuss the market potential, what problems it solves and benefits to both the licensee and end buyer it offers.

One of my clients asked their customers to show how they used their product, which generated some great product testimonials. These videos helped them get a deal with an international licensing partner.

Record these videos and post them on YouTube and other video sites. Keep it short - no more than three to four minutes – and to the point. If a picture tells 1000 more words, a video can tell a million words. It's one of the best ways to present your licensing opportunity.

Whether in the form of a webcast, podcast, or YouTube video, digital media offers excellent vehicles for marketing your licensing opportunity. Remember, the better a potential partner understands your IP and how they can make money with it, the more likely it is that they will license your intellectual property.

Meet and Greet at Trade Shows

The last tactic is what I call "meet and greet." There is nothing more effective than one-on-one meetings with potential licensing partners.

If you're ready to make presentations to a lot of potential licensing partners, then consider getting your trade show booth or sharing one. If it's a big trade show, then sharing space is a better option because new companies with small booths wind up in the less traveled areas of the show.

One of my toy clients used this strategy when they launched their product. They rented a small section of a bigger booth, which gave them high visibility, and they quickly caught the eye of some major entertainment studios and retail buyers. Sharing a booth gives you a better location, it's more cost effective, and you get more visibility.

Trade shows are also a great online marketing opportunity. Visit their website or social media pages. Sign up and start communicating with show attendees. You can promote your IP and set up meetings with interested companies. Add them to your email lists and send information and news about your IP. You can also buy lists of attendees and send them invitations to visit you at your booth.

One final and important point. If you're going to present your licensing opportunity, make sure it's to the right person. That's usually not a salesperson. They are focused on one thing, and that's selling. You want to connect with someone in the marketing department, business development, or brand management. And trade shows are a great place to get face time with these people. Relationships get results, and trade shows are one of the best ways to build those relationships.

Summary of Key Points

The first step to taking action with your IP can be intimidating. But don't let your lack of knowledge or understanding stop you. The most important thing you can do is get into action. Remember, an IP in motion makes money. Unless you do something with your IP, nothing will happen.

Every day you wait to do something with your IP, it costs you money - in legal fees, lost opportunities, or unrealized income. But if you don't map out a plan of how to get there, your odds of succeeding are low.

Taking action with your IP requires using different tools to reach licensing partners. These include a focused outreach email campaign, promoting through PR, using digital media to demonstrate your IP, presenting at trade shows, and providing timely information so potential partners can make educated decisions about your licensing opportunity.

Developing a licensing deal takes time (so does finding a partner which I discuss in the next chapter), especially if your target licensees are large companies. That's why it's crucial to create a plan with a list of potential licensees and contact them all. The best way to avoid getting stalled while trying to get a licensing deal is to keep your IP out there and in play with several potential partners, until one or more of them decide to commit to your licensing agreement.

Now, this is not to say that you should pit one potential licensing partner against the other - that is not good business. But you can let them know that you are presenting your IP to other companies and the reasons why you think they are a good fit as a licensing partner.

A licensing plan is not a "set and then forget it" document. You'll get lots of feedback (or no response) from potential partners, and you'll use this information to fine-tune your plan. Sometimes the lack of response is just as valuable as getting a response. It can lead you to discover the right industry or companies for your intellectual property.

And most important, always remember it's not how good your IP is, it's how good your ACTION is with your IP. It's what you do to promote, present, and sell your licensing opportunity that makes the difference between success and failure.

CHAPTER 9

Finding the Right Partner Takes Time

One of the most popular food brand franchises spent years looking for the right partner for their first licensed product. But it wasn't easy. It took lots of research and time searching for the right partner with the marketing resources to make it a success at retail. And it paid off. Within one year, sales of their first licensed product exceeded $150 million.

Finding the right licensing partners is challenging. It requires time, research, and due diligence. Sometimes this is a tricky process. For example, if you've developed a breakthrough technology that requires creating a market, finding the right type of partner is not exactly straightforward. If your IP is an incremental improvement to a current product or technology, you'll know who to approach in the market. But, there is a more efficient process. The trick is to know where to look.

Search Engines and News Feeds

The Internet is a great starting point for quick research. It's one of the first resources I use to find potential licensing partners. You can begin your search on the Internet by going to Google and Yahoo!, typing in a broad search word, and then narrow it down from there. Start with general search terms, such as "toys" or "medical devices," to find companies and their websites. You can dig down from there and start to qualify them.

Browse Google News to stay up to date with different industries and companies. Use Advanced News Search to make the process easier and faster by setting up automatic search alerts to find and send the information to you. For example, when you set up news searches on Google, they will automatically send you a summary list of the latest news articles about the industry or company.

Some tips for setting up news alerts are combining the word "licensing" with a specific industry, such as "toy licensing" or "food & beverage licensing." You can do the same thing with specific companies (e.g., "Big Toy Company licensing"). Setting up a search is also a great way to learn about competitive IP's. Try different variations of describing your IP, such as "payment and process" or "payment technology."

Set up a spreadsheet and list the companies you find. Be sure to save the search results URLs. It's a quick way to index information, and from there, you can dig down and start to qualify them.

Trade Magazines

There are trade magazines for everything - toys, apparel, gifts, stationery, auto repair, oil refinery - you name it - there's a trade magazine for it. There are even trade magazines for licensing and intellectual property.

Trade magazines are a great tool for fine-tuning your industry search. Remember when looking through these magazines that they're not consumer-oriented. They focus on the trade, meaning that they discuss industry issues and specific companies. Reading through these magazines will give you a good sense of who the companies are, what they produce, and where they distribute. You can find many of these trade magazines online or at several trade magazine portals such as freetrademagazinesource.com.

LinkedIn

LinkedIn is one of the best research tools you can use to find the right company. It's also one of the fastest ways to contact potential licensing partners. LinkedIn is my first go-to tool for all of my client assignments. I've used it to license all types of IP, from major entertainment movie franchises to new product inventions.

LinkedIn offers several great ways to search for prospects. One of the most powerful is the Industry and Company search. You can begin with a general industry search, such as "food and beverage." The search results will show you companies, contacts, and groups that are directly or indirectly in that industry.

From there, you can check each of the company's profiles to find out if they're potentially a good fit. The profile will give you a general summary of the company, their products or services and who their customers are, as well as a link to their company website.

Finding the Right Contact on LinkedIn

Identifying companies that might be right is only the first half of the puzzle. The second and sometimes the most challenging half, is finding the right person to contact at the company. Sending licensing information to the wrong contact leads nowhere.

The Company search is also a fast way to find all the people on LinkedIn who work at a company. You can view their profile summary and based on their job title and summary, and decide whether it makes sense to contact them. You'll also find links to published articles, research papers, and industry presentations to further qualify the contact.

Depending on the company, it could be someone in marketing, business development, or R&D. That's often one of the biggest challenges with licensing - finding the right contact. Consumer products and technology companies often have both inbound and outbound licensing executives. If you're targeting Fortune 500 industrial companies, R&D and Business Development executives are an excellent place to start. In smaller companies, it's likely the head of marketing or product development.

Let me share with you a story of how useful this search feature is. I was licensing a new reduced-fat cooking technology for the quick service restaurant industry. Initially, I targeted fast food restaurants. I thought 'this is a no-brainer for them.' After two months of getting no response from any of these companies, I figured out they weren't the right ones to contact.

I did some more research and came across a profile with a link to a conference where the executive gave a presentation on fat reducing oil technologies. After reading the presentation, I knew this was the right person to contact. I sent an introduction email and received a fast response requesting more information about the IP. As it turned out, the fast food companies outsourced their menu innovation (that's the term they use for developing new food items) to the large food production and chicken processing companies.

Now I knew the best bets were people in R&D, innovation, and food research. I ran a search for any job titles that contained R&D or innovation. As it turned out, they were the right execs to target, and I successfully presented to over a dozen global food production, chicken processing, and ingredient companies.

Using LinkedIn Groups to Find Licensing Partners

Similar to searching for companies and people, you can search for groups targeting specific types of industries, job functions, and even alumni. Groups also help you find contacts inside companies. LinkedIn identifies members in the group who are in your network, and you can find members inside specific companies.

You'll find groups for just about every industry and business, from consumer goods to biotech, entertainment, automotive, financial - the list is endless. And it's one of your best tools on LinkedIn. Through groups, you can engage with the community by sharing articles, videos, and other information about your licensing opportunity.

Here's how I use groups. Going back to the previous food technology licensing story, I joined several groups focused on the food and beverage industry, restaurants, and food preparation (chefs). In one group, I shared a blog post about the IP and received several responses requesting more information about it.

Other approaches I've used include explaining how the IP solves specific problems, comparing its benefits over the competition, and even a request to get feedback on the IP. But don't sell - tell about the IP and its value. Your goal is to connect with potential licensing partners, interact, and create interest in your IP.

Keeping Track

Be sure to keep track of who you contacted through LinkedIn. Include the person's name, title, and a link to their profile. I organize it by the company and use it to track all my communications with each contact. Having a live link to their profile makes it easy to quickly refer back to get more information about the contact or company.

Trade Shows

Another great source for finding your partners is trade shows (which I mentioned in the previous chapter) which happen everywhere. Trade shows are an efficient and fast way to learn about an industry and meet potential partners. It's an excellent opportunity to see their products and talk to their sales reps.

One of my clients invented a new hair care product. It was an accessory for curling irons. The first thing we did was go to a beauty trade show to evaluate possible licensing partners. We met companies in person, viewed their products, and learned who to contact regarding licensing.

We also got feedback on the IP. You can do this informally (which we did) such as asking them if they do any licensing. If so, you can then ask if they would be interested in licensing your IP. If they are interested, keep your pitch short with general information such as "the IP is a new hair accessory item." From there, you can find out what information they need, who to send it to and then follow-up with more specific information about your IP.

The most important opportunity that trade shows offer is networking. They have evening and morning events where you can meet people informally, and start to develop a relationship.

Meeting your potential licensing partners in person lets you quickly learn whether they are right for your intellectual property. In one case, I found an international distributor for a client who ultimately wound up licensing them their product.

There are trade shows for just about any product, service, or technology. Most of the trade shows offer websites where you can find out what companies are exhibiting and learn more about the industry. Two excellent resources to find out about trade shows are www.tsnn.com and www.expodatabase.com.

Trade Directories

Trade directories are a resource for statistics and information about companies in any industry anywhere in the world, from blow molding to vacuum pumps. On-line directories, such as Hoovers and Thompson, offer databases with detailed information about a company, including operations, products, locations, etc. You can search for industry-specific and regional directories as well.

Many of these directories allow you to do the first search for no fee. Some of these are free and some paid. Visit a local library and get access to most of these databases for free.

Summary of Key Points

Finding the right licensing partner is one of the most challenging and time-consuming. Looking for a licensing partner is like looking for a job. The search is a process of gathering information and contacts until you find the one that works for you.

The secret to finding the right partner is using the right resources. These save you time, money, and lots of frustration trying to figure out the right companies to contact. The more sources you use, the faster you'll find the right type of licensing partner.

The Internet is a good starting point for doing an initial search. Browse Google News to stay up to date with different industries and companies. Use the advanced news search to make the process easier and faster by setting up automatic search alerts to find and send the information to you.

LinkedIn offers many great ways to search for prospects. One of the most powerful is the Industry and Company search. From there you can check each of the company's profiles to find out if they're potentially a good fit.

Trade shows are an opportunity to meet a lot of potential licensees. When you meet your potential licensing partners in person, you can quickly learn whether they are right for your intellectual property.

You can also read trade magazines for a specific industry, such as apparel or toys, and learn about potential candidates. Trade magazines are a great tool for fine-tuning your industry search.

You don't have to restrict your search to your backyard. Some of your best licensing opportunities could be in other countries around the world.

CHAPTER 10

One Size Doesn't Fit All

Getting stuck with a bad licensing partner is a legal nightmare I've seen many times. In one case, it was two inventor partners who licensed their technology exclusively to the first company that offered them a deal. They didn't bother researching the company to verify its capabilities. It turned out the company was nothing more than a name, and the person they were dealing with had no money or resources to do anything with their IP. The problem was they were stuck in a five-year deal and couldn't get their IP rights back without a legal fight.

If you don't research a partner before signing the licensing deal, you can wind up working with a company who lacks the resources or doesn't have the skills to manage and get your IP into the market. Or worse, a company who is dishonest in the way they use your IP and fail to pay you.

Due Diligence Advantage

Once you've found a partner interested in licensing your IP, the next step is the due diligence process. Don't overlook this step because it's a critical one. It's the process of qualifying a partner by getting as much information as needed to make sure they have the money, people, and resources to get your IP into the market.

When I was licensing kid's movies and TV shows, the first thing every potential licensee had to complete was a licensee application. It included references for retail buyers, distribution, and banking, which I always checked. Plus they had to provide their marketing plan detailing their go-to-market strategy and timelines.

You'll also want to find out about a partner's experience with licensing. However, experience with licensing should not necessarily be required. Often licensing is a new strategy for a company, which means your IP would be the only fish in the pond.

Most important, confirm if the potential partner has the financial resources, especially if the company is a startup. They usually don't have lots of money, and if sales for your IP take off and they can't fill the orders, it will hurt your IP and potentially cause customers (both retail and end users) to back away from buying it.

Other areas to research include the quality of their products (or services), company reputation, distribution capabilities, and whether or not they sell competing products. If possible, speak with other IP owners working with the company to get as much insight into them as possible. Researching a large public company is much easier. Since they must report everything, there are many resources you can use, including annual reports, SEC filings, news reports, and investment reports.

Make sure your IP "fits" the licensee. If your patented product requires complex electronic components, a company that produces only injection-molded plastic products is not right for your product. The same holds down the line - from production through distribution channels. Don't license a product with high production costs and a high retail price to a company that specializes in products that are under $8 and sell at the cash register. It's not the right fit - they don't have the experience or resources for that market, and most likely will not succeed in getting your IP into the commercial market.

Why Size Matters

When I was licensing the kid's entertainment properties, many of the early licensees were small companies willing to take a risk. Nobody knew if the property would hit with the kids. Retail orders initially were small. Then suddenly, when the property got hot, the retailers ordered large quantities to meet the surge in demand. It overwhelmed the production capabilities of many licensees, who tried to quickly ramp up production. Some were able to meet the demand, and many didn't have the resources to fill the orders.

Market size is a critical factor in evaluating potential licensing partners. A $200 million market is pocket change to a large corporation, but they move slowly. Smaller companies are often speedy and agile but don't have the capabilities of a larger firm.

Although a smaller company may fit in every other area, you have a choice to make: trade-off a good fit and the prospect of a good working relationship for access to a broader market. If the market for your IP is national, it's better to find a larger licensing partner or one that has access to the national marketplace.

And finally, when considering a licensing partner, look beyond the number one player. Consider whether the number one company needs your IP or whether the number two or three player can benefit in much more significant ways.

4 Qualification Questions

To help you qualify potential licensing partners, here's a checklist with the four key areas to research before entering a licensing agreement:

1. Quality and Reputation of the Licensee. Does the licensee meet with your quality standards and is in good standing with its distribution channels, retail partners, and customers?

2. Experience of the Licensee. Does your type of IP fit within their product or service line and sales channels?

3. Financial Condition of the Licensee. Does the licensee have the financial resources needed to succeed with your IP?

4. Competing Products. If so, will the licensee devote enough resources and attention to your IP?

Once the research is complete, make sure that you can work with the licensee. It's vital that you and your licensing partners share the same vision or goals for your IP.

The more you and your potential licensing partner know about each other, the better you can decide if the partnership makes sense.

Summary of Key Points

The right licensing partner can make or break your licensing program. It requires finding a partner with the capabilities to get it right, who knows the industry and understands your goals for your IP.

Be sure to qualify the potential licensing partner and verify they have the right capabilities, such as R&D, manufacturing, and distribution already in place. If your IP is competitive to their products or services, take that into account. The better your IP fits a company's capabilities, the more likely they'll succeed in the marketplace.

It also reduces the risk your partner won't perform. If your IP is a "mass market product" then a potential licensee must have national distribution capabilities. Although a smaller company may fit in every other area, mass market demand can overwhelm their production capabilities. It's better to find a bigger licensing partner who can handle the market demand.

Spending a little time doing some research and qualifying your potential partner will save you lots of time and headaches down the road, and go a long way in making sure you create the right licensing partnership.

CHAPTER 11

Telling the Right Story

When a well-known celebrity brand wanted to expand into furniture, it required more than just a bunch of images. It needed a story - not just any story, but a story that positioned it like one of the big lifestyle brands representing a particular way of life. They created a story showcasing furniture designs that connected with their huge fan base of potential customers and persuaded retail buyers to sell the products. That story presented a big licensing opportunity which convinced several furniture companies to license the brand.

When it comes to licensing, how you say it is just as important as what you say. If you want to get a licensing deal, your licensing presentation must look like a great licensing opportunity. The best way to do this is to make sure you're telling the right story of why your intellectual property is valuable to a licensing partner.

4 Common Mistakes That Can Sink Your Licensing Presentation

A big part of success is licensing is creating the right kind of presentation. Get it right, and your licensing partner wants to know more. Get it wrong, and they'll walk away. Here's a list of the top 4 mistakes when presenting your licensing opportunity and how to avoid them.

1. Including confidential information in the initial presentation.

Any information included in this presentation must be non-confidential (see the earlier chapter on Getting Ready). Don't include trade secrets, know-how, source code, proprietary processes, systems, or anything else that is confidential. If you're not sure, then don't include it.

It's the first information you're showing a potential licensing partner. Most companies won't sign an NDA at this initial stage until they know whether or not they are interested in your IP. I've spoken with many inventors who try to get an NDA signed before providing any information about their IP. They meet with a "no" from the potential licensing partner who refuses to sign one. That's understandable considering they don't even know what the IP is. Communication with the potential licensee grinds to a halt and the inventor winds up with nothing to show for all their time invested in getting the company interested in their IP.

The right time to provide confidential information is after a potential licensing partner is interested and wants to learn about the "secret sauce" inside your IP. At that point, getting a signed confidential disclosure agreement is necessary before you give them the information. But not before.

2. Failing to show your IP in a tangible format.

It's tough to present your IP with just words. The problem is what you say is often interpreted differently than what you mean. Plus, if the IP is very complex, explaining it can get very confusing, especially if you're presenting to non-technical execs, such as marketing or sales. If they don't understand it, they won't be interested in licensing it.

Videos, animation, and 3D printing are some ways to create a "tangible" sample of your IP. If it's new technology such as an algorithm or software, show images of exactly what the technology is and how it works. One of my clients developed a frequency technology used for non-medical treatments, such as post-surgery healing. They produced short videos showing how the technology was embedded in a variety of sounds so patients could "hear" the technology working.

If you're presenting a prototype or early production sample, don't build it for you. Build if for your licensing partners. Use components, housing, screens, and sensors - whatever it requires - that are off the shelf, meaning parts produced and used in similar products. Licensees don't like to reinvent the wheel, especially when it comes to production. It's a common problem in licensing. It's also one of the biggest reasons many IP owners are unsuccessful in licensing their IP. If a potential partner thinks your product or device will be too expensive to make and requires a complete "re-do" to produce it, they'll most likely pass.

If it's a trademark or copyright, demonstrate it by applying it to the potential licensee's product. When I was at the studios licensing the entertainment properties, we always created a style guide with artwork showing the property on different types of products. The artwork was easy to use in customizing presentations to potential licensing partners' products. If it was a t-shirt company, the presentation included images of the characters on different types of t-shirts so they could "see" what the property looked like on their products.

A prototype that clearly illustrates the functionality, creativity and utility of your IP is your most essential tool. We live in a tangible world and the impact of being able to hold and try a new product vs. describing it is substantial.

3. Using the Wrong Format

Don't just walk in with brochures, diagrams or other materials. If it's not organized and presented in a format that is easy to show and follow, they'll lose interest quickly.

PowerPoint is one of the best formats to use (more on this later in this chapter). Focus on the market potential, what problems your IP solves, and benefits it offers to both the licensee and to end customers.

If your IP is still in development, you can show pictures, diagrams or animation. Include any production cost estimates, testimonials you've collected, and any other materials that help demonstrate the potential your IP has in the marketplace...but don't include any confidential information.

4. Failing to Explain Why Your IP is Better

Don't spend all your time talking about the technical details of your IP, and nothing about why it's better, faster or cheaper than the competition. You have to prove your IP's value (if you missed that chapter, go back and read it now).

Just because you get it registered as copyright or trademark or receive a patent doesn't mean the IP is worth anything. Unless it works - increases revenue or lowers costs, provides a competitive advantage, or does something cheaper, faster, and better - it isn't worth anything.

The best thing that you can do to succeed in licensing is to validate your technology or your product. The better you can document this - the more you can prove why it's better, faster, or cheaper - the higher the likelihood you'll succeed in licensing.

Remember a potential partner must understand why your IP is worth the risk of licensing it. If a licensee doesn't understand why your IP is unique and how they'll make money with it, they won't be interested.

5 Keys to a Successful Presentation

The goal of your presentation is to get a "yes we're interested" answer. Create a concise presentation and tell the right story. To help you make the best impression, here's a list of 5 keys to a successful licensing presentation:

1. Keep it Simple

Even if your IP is very technical, don't make your presentation "tech-heavy." Remember, you will most likely be sending it to marketing, sales, and product development folks.

I recommend using PowerPoint with lots of images and minimal text. Keep it to 8 - 10 slides. Any more and you'll lose people's attention. The idea of a PowerPoint is not to get into the nitty-gritty detail, but to present the big picture and market opportunity for your IP.

Make sure to use images that reinforce the story you're telling and how your IP solves a big problem (and makes a lot of money doing it). For example, if it's a new software technology show it along with images of companies who will use it. If it's a new consumer product, show it with pictures of customers and where they would buy it. If it's a brand, show how it looks on lots of different products.

If you're presenting in person, use your due-diligence research to support why and how the IP fits their business model.

Ask some questions before starting the presentation to see if anything has changed, and if so, and then adjust your presentation based on that updated information.

2. Show them the Money ⟵

In almost every presentation I've made, one of the first questions asked is, "Will the IP make money"?

When it comes to licensing, nothing sells the deal like numbers promising future success. Numbers paint a more compelling picture than words about the market opportunity. Show numbers early and often – and be ready to prove their validity. I like to use graphs to show the numbers. It's easier to grasp and show than a bunch of numbers on a spreadsheet.

Don't over-hype the numbers. It's a mistake many IP owners make. Nothing puts off a potential licensing partner faster than a lot of hot air hype.

3. Focus on What Matters

Don't veer off on the road of irrelevancy and into blind alleys of pointlessness. Here is an example of the difference between something you focus on and what is irrelevant in your licensing presentation. "Our IP is featured in XYZ Magazine's 100 Coolest Things of the Year special." That is worth focusing on because it demonstrates a genuine public interest in the products or services created from your IP.

Now, by contrast, here is something you don't focus on in your licensing presentation. "It took six months to develop the prototype." It doesn't matter how long it took, and quite frankly, they don't care. What matters is does it work and fits with their business. By staying laser-focused, you lead the potential licensee down the road of wanting to license your IP.

4. Make it Logical

Deliver the presentation in a logical sequence, with each slide or point building upon earlier ones.

I've met with inventors who immediately start telling me how much their invention will make before describing their invention. Don't start talking about projected sales and profit before explaining the IP. If the potential licensee doesn't know how or what your IP does, your numbers won't make sense, plus you'll wind up explaining them again once they understand the IP.

5. Keep it Short

You're not telling your life story. Your licensing partner is only interested in one thing - making money with your IP. Keep it under 20 minutes. Any more and you'll lose people's attention. Remember, potential licensing partners are running a business. Their time is valuable, and unless you get right to the point, they'll quickly lose interest.

Summary of Key Points

The goal of your presentation is to get a "yes we're interested" answer. Your presentation must be concise and tell the right story. It must engage your potential licensing partner and demonstrate the value your IP brings to their business.

Be energetic and deliver your presentation with passion. Do your homework, and make sure your IP fits the licensees business. Most importantly, make sure you detail how and why they'll make money with your IP.

The one thing I want to stress here is don't give up. Not every company is going to find your IP attractive or right. I can't tell you how many times I've worked on a property where "No" was the only answer I got. Then something changed either in the company such as new management, or in the market such as new legal regulations, and suddenly it was a "Yes." Timing is everything, and "No" is rarely a definitive answer because the marketplace for intellectual properties is so dynamic.

Don't get discouraged!

CHAPTER 12

You Get the Deal You Negotiate

Several years ago, one of my clients retained me to help them get international rights to some popular kid's entertainment franchises. In one situation, we were negotiating with a large toy company for several of their top shows. We negotiated the terms for the deal with their representatives in the country we wanted rights to, and after we finished they sent a deal term sheet confirming the terms we agreed to.

We waited for several months and didn't hear from the company about the licensing agreement. Then one day we received an email explaining that there's been a change and new management is in place. And now we had to re-negotiate the deal terms they agreed to with the new person.

The First Rule of Negotiating

The first rule of negotiating is patience. The timing is dependent on so many variables, such as the type of IP, the parties involved, the rights, whether it has to go through multiple departments, to name a few. I've negotiated deals in as little as two weeks. In other cases, it took two years to finish negotiating the licensing agreement.

78

There's the people factor to consider. I've worked on licensing deals where we started with one person, only to find out months later they had left the company. When this happens, you can wind up starting over with the new person. In other cases, the company might reorganize and move the licensing to a different person, division, or county. Then there are meetings, vacations, sick days and holidays, all of which add time to completing the licensing deal.

If your IP is disruptive, such as a new technology that revolutionizes an industry, or a complicated deal, it's going to take longer to close. The bigger the company, the slower they are when it comes to negotiating a licensing agreement. Especially if they are negotiating international rights, which is complicated because of their various divisions in each territory, and each one has to make sure there is no conflict with other deals. It's usually a painfully slow process, and fundamental to getting the deal closed is diligently following up to make sure they don't drop the ball.

Generally, the only way you can use time urgency to close a licensing deal faster is with a competing offer, a pending event (such as a movie release), or there is only a short window of opportunity in the market.

Be Prepared

Negotiating terms is sometimes the trickiest part of a licensing deal. It's a back and forth process of figuring out the best business terms for your partnership. Sometimes negotiations go smoothly. Other times it can be a real nightmare.

When you think you've finished negotiating the terms, you get an email asking for one small change on what you agreed to. Then another email requesting a different change followed by another email and still another. It is known as nibbler negotiation, and it's a tactic used to slowly change the terms of the agreement.

In one deal, I negotiated a deal with a huge hair care company and agreed they would get the professional salon market. Two weeks later they sent an email saying they wanted to expand the distribution channels to include consumers because the market is bigger. We thought it over and agreed to their request. A few days later, another email arrived, this time changing the royalty rate because the product was still unknown, and they felt that a loyal lower royalty rate was warranted. We went back and forth for quite some time and became very frustrating.

The better prepared you are for negotiations, the better you'll be able to stop this tactic. To do that requires knowing what your bottom line terms are for the licensing agreement. That way you'll be ready to say no if the licensee continues to nibble away. That's what happened with the hair care company. It got to the point where what they were offering wasn't worth doing the deal.

Always remember the goal of negotiating to make it a win-win deal. Do your homework and know what terms you're willing to accept. But if your potential partner continues to nibble away at the deal terms, it's better to step away before they eat up your deal.

The Most Important Deal Point

As you're negotiating, never lose sight that the right partner is the most critical deal point. Your negotiations are about what you and your licensing partner will do to make your IP successful in the marketplace. It's not one team trying to get an advantage over the other. If you feel as though a partner is seeking an advantage over you, don't sign the agreement. If the negotiations turn adversarial, then it's time to reconsider your partner. Otherwise, you will end up in a bad relationship that will be very difficult to manage, and it will be challenging to try to fix the situation, especially if the contract is one-sided.

You're negotiating a long-term agreement. Be clear and concise about what those terms are. If your potential licensing partner cannot give what you need to make a license work, no matter how harmonious your visions, no matter how well you seem able to get along, the agreement will fail.

Dealing with Difficult Issues

Part of the negotiation process is dealing with the difficult issues up front. Not everybody is going to agree on everything, but all the issues have to get out on the table.

One of these is money - what is the royalty rate, how much is the guarantee, and when will it be paid. Other sticky areas include exclusivity, who owns what IP rights in development, the option to renew (sometimes automatically), and when and how the agreement terminates.

Sometimes these aren't difficult issues if you're negotiating with a big company or institution, because they use standard terms for all their agreements, with little or no negotiating. When I was licensing entertainment properties, if the movie or TV show was hot, it required a six-figure (or above) minimum guarantee for the license.

You want to make sure you get it right because I can tell you, a bad deal is worse than no deal at all. Even if you think you've successfully negotiated a fair deal, always review it with an experienced licensing attorney before signing it to make sure it's a win-win deal for both you and your licensing partner.

Why You Shouldn't Negotiate Your Deal

The number one reason it's not a good idea to negotiate yourself is you aren't objective about your intellectual property. To be successful, you have to remain objective. But you can't do that when it's your IP. It's your baby. You tend to get emotional when something said about your IP isn't positive. Critical questions about whether your IP will work trigger an emotional response as if they had insulted you.

Another big issue when negotiating yourself is becoming over-anxious about wanting to get the deal closed. You start making concessions or overlook performance milestones, only to realize later these come back to bite you. You agree to include the international market rights to get the deal closed without specifying a marketing date. One year later, the licensing partner still hasn't launched your IP into the global market. But now you're locked into this agreement, and you've got limited options for getting your rights back without spending lots of time and money on legal action.

The best thing you can do to avoid falling into these traps is to hire the services of a licensing agent (such as myself) or attorney to negotiate a deal for you. They're objective and will focus on getting the best deal for your IP. Most importantly, they keep you out of trouble.

Closing Your First Licensing Deal

Getting the first licensing partner on board is always a big challenge. Here's a negotiating strategy that's one of the best ways to do that. It's called the sweetheart deal. The approach is simple - offer your first partner a license at little or no cost up front. It is a good strategy if you can license more than one partner for your IP.

Since you've got a lot riding on the success of your first licensee, it's smart for you to put a lot of time and help in getting your licensing partner started. Once you have the first licensee on board, it will attract other licensing partners. There's nothing that sells a licensing deal faster than an active licensing partner (especially if they are a large company) who is a reference for other licensees.

I consulted a client who created an event brand for nightclubs. They wanted to license the brand to nightclubs to create events and attract new customers. When they approached me, a night club who heard about their brand contacted them. We negotiated the first license using the sweetheart deal. No upfront money in return for the night club promoting the brand and the event. The result was a big hit and lots of publicity. It kick-started their licensing program and it attracted several large nightclub operators who wanted to license their event brand for multiple locations.

Whether your IP is a product, service, brand, or technology, if you are looking for a fast way to get your first licensing partner use the sweetheart deal. That doesn't mean they are not a paying partner; it means no upfront costs and they pay you royalties on sales. It's a win-win for everyone.

Summary of Key Points

Successful negotiation is all about preparation. If you're not ready, you wind up flopping all over the place whipsawed by different discussions, giving away the store, getting a lower royalty rate, and a host of other terms that you later regret agreeing to simply because you weren't ready to discuss them.

Put together a list of key business terms, such as IP rights, territories, exclusivity, royalty rate, etc. Decide what you must have and what you're willing to compromise.

Consider using a third-party, such as a licensing agent or attorney. They'll be objective, are experienced in negotiating agreements, they will keep you out of trouble.

Be patient. Negotiations take time. Sometimes they move quickly, and other times it can take months or years. Your licensing deal is only one of many tasks your licensing partner is managing. How long it takes depends on the IP, how responsive each partner is, and how complicated the licensing deal terms are.

Make sure you confirm the business terms agreed to with a written term sheet such as a deal memo, e-mail, or short form letter agreement. Don't wait until the 40-page long form arrives; you may find that the deal you thought you made isn't a deal at all.

The first licensing partner is always the most challenging because they are taking the biggest risk, especially if your IP is unknown or still needs development. Offering a sweetheart deal for little or no money upfront is one of the best ways to encourage your first licensing partner to license your IP. They help validate your IP and attract other licensing partners, especially if they are a big company.

And finally, always remember, you don't get the licensing deal you deserve; you get the licensing deal you negotiate.

CHAPTER 13

Royalty Rate Myths and Mistakes

Royalty rates are one of the most mystifying and least understood areas of licensing. Many IP owners get caught up in trying to get the highest royalty rate or the most money up front instead of looking for the right deal that will generate the most money.

A royalty rate is not the value of the IP. In a licensing deal, the royalty rate is the formula that calculates how much the licensee will pay the IP owner for the rights to use the intellectual property. The more critical or significant intellectual property is to revenue and profitability, the higher the royalty rate.

But that's not the only thing that determines the royalty rate. Other things impacting the royalty rate include IP development, production costs, profitability, competitive IPs, legal issues, regulatory approvals, and more.

To help take the mystery out of royalty rates, let's take a look at four royalty rate myths, and separate the fact from fiction.

Myths and Mistakes

A high value means a high royalty rate.

The best IP always makes the most money.

The bigger the innovation is, the higher the royalty rate.

These are just some of the myths and misconceptions about royalty rates. This type of thinking is often applied by IP owners when trying to negotiate a licensing deal. So now I'll dispel some of the biggest myths, and share with you some real-world tips on figuring out a royalty rate for your licensing agreements.

Myth #1: The standard royalty rate.

There is no one "standard" rate for any IP. Look into royalty rates for your type of intellectual property, and you'll most likely find a range or average, but not a specific rate. Contrary to popular belief, royalty rates are negotiable.

When I was at the studios, even if a movie or TV show was hot and the going royalty rate was "12%" it varied by each product category. If it was a high-profit margin product category, such as toys, the royalty rate was closer to 12%, but for a low-profit-margin product category, such as publishing, the royalty rate was 5%.

Terms of your licensing agreement also affect the royalty rates. Some of the most valuable rights include exclusivity, multiple types of IP (i.e., patents, know-how, copyrights, and technical data), rights to future improvements, and rights to sub-license. Other factors that impact the royalty rate include demand for the IP and the negotiation skills of the licensee and licensor.

Myth #2: There is an inherent value for certain types of IP.

Not every IP is valuable. A royalty rate does not equal the value of intellectual property. It is a formula to calculate the amount of the revenue stream paid to the property owner. Much of it depends on whether it is market tested, generating revenues, or still needs development.

If its potential to generate revenues is not known, its value remains a question mark. A raw idea isn't worth anything because its risk is astronomical. If an IP still needs a significant amount of development, the royalty rate will be lower. If it's close to being market ready or it's in the market, the royalty rate will be higher.

Kid's movies are a good example. When I was at the studio licensing the first Batman movie, no major company was interested. It hadn't been seen for 20 years, and it was an "unknown" (except to comic book fans) property with significant risk. The companies that did take the risk were licensing it for about 5%. When the movie launched and became a big hit, the royalty rate quickly skyrocketed to 10% and higher.

Myth #3: The bigger the innovation, the bigger the royalty.

Again, it's a question of cost versus profitability. If you've got a complex patented product or device that takes millions of dollars and years to build, with low margins, the royalty rate will be lower because the risk is very high and the profit margins are not there.

Many great IPs are developed only to discover later (usually when the IP owner tries to license it) that it's not commercially viable – meaning it isn't as profitable as the IP owner thought. It depends on all sorts of variables, such as whether your IP is ready for market, the cost to make (or deliver), whether it is a breakthrough technology, and many more.

Myth #4: The best technology makes the most successful products.

Not necessarily the case. Generally, it's the first to market that makes the most revenue. In many cases, inventors spend an excessive amount of time trying to perfect their IP when, in reality, what they should be doing is bringing it to market.

There are many case studies of products that come to market less than 100% ready (such as computer software), yet do very well because the owners brought it into the market quickly, while continually improving it. Most often, the first to market makes the most money, generally captures the highest revenue share, and establishes the number one place in the market. You don't want to spend a significant amount of time trying to tweak and fine tune an intellectual property that's ready to go to market.

Types of Royalty Payments

Royalties are the term used for licensing payments, and there are different ways to calculate these payments. Some of the most common is a lump sum, running royalties (also known as a percentage royalty), fixed amounts, and tiered royalties. The royalty rate doesn't have to be the same for the term of the agreement. Which formula you use depends on your IP.

Lump Sum is a single payment, usually paid one time or annually, and it's generally not tied to any sales or performance benchmarks. It's frequently used with unknown technologies when sales are hard to project, or in mature markets (commodity type of products with lots of competition, such as electronics) where the profit margins are very low.

Running or percentage royalties use sales to calculate the amount of each payment, such as 6% of gross sales. It's best for "product" based licenses, such as inventions, movies, and brands. Because this formula uses the selling price, if your IP becomes wildly successful in the marketplace, it will generate big financial rewards to both you and your licensing partner. The licensing deals I did while at the studios use this formula, and when these properties suddenly took off in the market, the royalty revenues skyrocketed right along with product sales, generating hundreds of millions of dollars in royalty revenues.

A fixed amount per unit royalty is best with new or unknown technology with high production costs and low profit margins. But keep in mind, this type of royalty is a cap on how much royalty the licensee will pay per sale. It doesn't automatically go up if the price increases.

Tiered or Volume Percentage is a royalty rate that moves up or down based on the sales or revenue volume of the licensee. For example, the royalty starts at 3% for sales revenue between 0 and $2 million, then increases by 1% at $2 million, and tops out at 5% for sales over $5 million. This formula is best for new technology or product that requires a lot of time and money to get it into the market, and the profit margins are unknown, such as launching in a foreign market.

When I negotiated several licensing deals for international rights to some famous movie franchises, we used the tiered royalty formula. The royalties increased based on reaching certain milestones, either a level of sales or on a specific date, whichever occurred first. It was a good compromise and gave my client a lower royalty initially to help recoup their investment in developing the property and provided the licensor a higher average royalty over the term of the license.

Summary of Key Points

A little homework before negotiating your licensing deal will help you figure out a starting point for the royalty rate. Many variables impact the royalty rate, such as the type of IP, its development stage, the market, and many others.

One of the most significant factors is the profit margin. What does it cost to generate sales and how much profit does the IP make? If the profit margins are low, then the royalty rates will be low. For example, basic or commodity type products, such as electronics, usually have low margins and need lower royalty rates. Conversely, a new innovative product with high-profit margins can get a higher royalty rate.

Keep in mind royalty rates are the price a licensing partner is willing to pay because of the financial return it offers them. The closer your IP is to being market ready, the higher the royalty rate. While there are "industry averages" and formulas, at the end of the day it comes down to what you and your licensing partner negotiate.

Remember that the best licensing deals are not about how much money you get paid up front, but how much money you get paid over the term of the licensing agreement.

CHAPTER 14

Use the Right Lease to Rent Your House

Before licensing your intellectual property, you must know what type of agreement you'll need. You wouldn't use a commercial lease to rent your one bedroom house. The same is true for licensing. Use the right agreement, and your partnership runs smoothly, but if you use the wrong one, you can wind up losing more than just your royalties.

The licensing agreement is a contract between you and your partner on what you agree to do to bring your IP to the market successfully. It's your plan, but it's also a written document designed to avoid litigation by anticipating what could go wrong. It spells out how potential problems are resolved, such as a dispute, or late payment, or not submitting a product for approval. It's also a document that will sometimes outlive the people who created the partnership. Memories fade or people change and unless it's in writing anybody new stepping in can stop or change the deal.

The market is always changing, which means your agreement may change as well. If your contract is explicit on how you resolve changing market conditions, such as delays in production, hitting the marketing date, or any number of changing market conditions, it keeps the relationship smooth and the license moving forward.

Movie studios are notorious for sudden management changes, which if it happens, can delay product approvals and market entry. One of my clients was licensing big movie franchises for rights in China. Part of our negotiating strategy was tying approval milestone terms to guarantee payments. Sure enough, a management change did happen with one of the studios, and approvals came to a standstill. The strategy paid off, and it saved my client from getting drained by the guarantee payments.

Licensing Agreements Take Time

Some agreements move quickly, while others can fall into a black hole and never get completed. It runs the scale, and it all depends on the type of intellectual property and the licensing partner. Movie licenses take a long time. TV deals are shorter. Inventor deals move along faster. Music deals can move slowly. Other things impacting the time include the nature of the IP owner (easy or difficult to deal with), the type of IP (a single product or new brain surgery technology), complexity of the license, and whether it involves other licensees.

Not every contract is necessarily complicated. It all depends on what kind of licensing deal you're doing. There are short form contracts and long form contracts. Sometimes the IP owner provides it, while in other situations the licensee gives it.

Then the agreement is reviewed and revisions discussed, which, is actually a series of negotiations. It's a back and forth communication between you and your licensing partner. Completing this process depends on how fast each of you responds. It continues until the revised agreement is acceptable to both of you.

The bigger the company, the slower the deal moves. In one case, I was finalizing agreement terms with one of the big studios for an international license, which further complicated the process because they had to run the agreement by other divisions in the different territories. Frequently, we spent weeks trying to schedule a date everyone was available to discuss unresolved issues. It was a painfully slow process that ran eighteen months before we finally signed the licensing agreement. It required diligently following up to make sure they didn't drop the ball.

Types of Licensing Agreements

Just like real estate, there are different types of agreements for renting or leasing IP. The most common types of licensing agreements include technology (patents), trademarks (merchandise), copyright, and trade secrets (know-how). Sometimes these agreements cover more than one type of IP. For example, a license for patent rights and manufacturing know-how is often called a "patent and know-how license agreement."

While there are parts of these agreements that are similar, there are some significant differences. Here's a quick summary of these licensing agreements and some of the main differences between them:

Patent License

Your patents are legal rights that only prohibit others from using the parts of your technology covered by the patent claims. A patent license allows your licensing partner to make, use, and sell something based on your patent claims in return for paying you royalties (as well as not getting sued for infringement).

A patent license is a performance-based agreement, and it's specific about milestone benchmarks and timelines, such as IP development, product testing, and regulatory approvals. If they don't make them, you have the right to end the agreement.

The common forms of patent licenses include exclusive, non-exclusive, and cross-licensing. An exclusive patent license is more valuable to the licensee than a non-exclusive license. For example, a new engine-related invention is licensed exclusively to different manufacturers in the airplane, motorcycle, and boat industries. Or it is licensed non-exclusively to different automobile manufacturers. It is also used to acquire rights to someone else's patent through a cross-licensing deal that "trades" the right to use each other's IP for no royalties.

In many cases, a patent license also includes trade secrets and know-how, such as manufacturing process, which can increase the value of the licensing deal.

Trademark License

A trademark license allows the licensee to use the brand or trademark to sell its products or services. The most significant difference between a trademark and patent or copyright license is the degree of control. The trademark license protects the quality and reputation of a trademark or brand by strictly controlling the look, design, type, and quality of products produced by your licensing partner. If you don't enforce your quality control terms, you risk not only damaging the value of your trademark but also possibly losing rights to it as well.

Copyright License

Copyrights are unique because they include six different rights (copy, edit/add, perform, print, distribute, reuse, produce) within the copyright itself. A copyright licensing agreement gives someone the limited right to use one or more of these rights for a specified period. Limited is critical. It restricts the use of other rights.

For instance, a book license gives the reproduction and distribution rights to a publisher, but not the rights to any derivatives (such as a TV show) or merchandise (such as toys). The publisher can only make, distribute, and sell copies of the book.

In the technology industry, copyrights protect software, and the licensing agreement limits how the software use, such as rights to the end-user business market, or only bundled under an OEM licensing agreement.

That's why the copyright licensing agreement must be particular about included rights as well as those rights not included. Otherwise, you can wind up in a dispute later when you try to license your copyright to other licensing partners.

Trade Secrets License

Trade secrets cover a diverse range of IP, including formulas, know-how, software, business systems, manufacturing processes, and all types of data such as information about suppliers, competitors, and customers.

Because trade secrets aren't registered, keeping it confidential is critical. A trade secret licensing agreement details specifically which information is confidential and which isn't, limits on its use, and details how long it must stay secret (usually for two to five years).

Trade secrets are licensed separately or combined with other types of IP, such as a patent (known as a hybrid agreement). In many cases, they enhance the value of the patent and can extend the life of the patent license agreement. Other options include licensing it as part of a consulting agreement, where you give your know-how to a company for use in their business.

Summary of Key Points

Before you start licensing your IP, make sure you know what type of agreement to use. The most common types of licensing agreements include technology (patents), trademarks (merchandise), copyright, and trade secrets (know-how).

The essential part of creating a licensing agreement is your partnership. The goal is a win-win relationship. It requires legal counsel and time to put together a clear and solid contract.

One of the worst things you can do is rush into it. That leads to a bad licensing deal. I can't emphasize this enough: a bad deal is worse than no deal at all. A bad agreement is tough to get out of without spending lots of time and money.

Once you sign the agreement, you want a productive and profitable experience for both you and your licensing partner. A licensing agreement creates a relationship that requires regular contact. While the "thanks very much, now send me my royalties" mentality is typical, it doesn't lead to a profitable relationship in the long run.

Keep contacts open and regular, and stay abreast of the latest developments. Call people. Keep an eye on things. At the very least, you will stand a smaller chance of being surprised.

CHAPTER 15

There is No Standard Licensing Deal

The wording of your licensing terms is critical. If your conditions aren't clear, it can wind up costing you lots of money or worse, losing control of your intellectual property.

One of the largest computer companies learned this lesson the hard way when they licensed their user interface design to a competitor. They thought they had limited its use to tiled images. But the clause wasn't specific enough, and they wound up with a competitor whose functionality looked identical to theirs.

I've spoken with many IP owners who have unknowingly signed away all their IP rights, and never gotten paid for the use of their IP or made next to nothing out of a license. That situation is entirely avoidable if you understand a few of the essential terms inside the licensing agreement and what to watch out for when negotiating these terms.

9 Key Licensing Agreement Terms

Most licensing agreements are similar as far as the nuts and bolts of the terms go. They specify how the partners get in, what each partner agrees to do, and how they get out. But there is no "standard licensing deal."

The licensing agreement reflects a unique set of circumstances, and the "standard terms" are always modified based on the goals and expectations of you and your licensing partner.

While there are many terms in licensing agreements, certain parts are vital to the success of a deal. I'll walk you through these key terms:

1. Market Rights

There are many ways of dividing up licensing rights. Fields of use (i.e., specific industry, application or use), products or product lines, marketing channels, and duration of license are just a few of the ways.

During my studio licensing days, we used to slice and dice the rights by product categories, territories, even distribution channels. If the property was hot, licensing partners came up with all sorts of new "products" to get a license. Sometimes these were minor variations of broader product categories, like action figures. In one case, a licensee created characters with big heads that wobbled (bobbleheads). Or they figured out a new distribution channel for a toy, such as through direct response.

The vital point to keep in mind is you must understand the different ways to license your IP. If it has potential applications in other markets, industries, products, or uses, don't give away the store by agreeing to license all the market rights to your IP. Be very specific on what the license can and can't do with your IP. Otherwise, you can wind up losing out on other licensing opportunities.

2. Duration of Agreement

How long the agreement runs depends on the type of intellectual property. Patents agreements generally run until the patent ends. Trademark agreement will go three to five years, with renewals based on performance. Copyright agreements run both long and short durations depending on the rights you are licensing. Book rights generally run the life of the copyright, but merchandise or promotions run only a few years. A longer-term agreement gives you guaranteed income, but it can change if the markets change. A short-term deal gives you a chance to test the partnership.

Length or duration also applies to specific rights within the agreement, such as exclusivity in a particular territory or for different products. And it's often tied to meeting performance milestones, such as marketing dates. I've worked with clients on deals where a licensee only has rights to a product for a limited time. If they didn't start selling it by a specific date, they lost rights to it, but the original contract duration remained active.

Duration is also flexible and can start on a short term basis with an option to extend it into a long term agreement. Using options to negotiate the length of a contract is common in situations where the IP still needs development and testing to confirm its market viability. When I was working with the client who invented a new patented fat reduction cooking process technology for fried foods (which I mentioned in an earlier chapter), it was untested in the commercial marketplace. In this case, potential licensing partners always asked whether my client was open to a two-phase licensing agreement. Phase one included a short-term period to test the IP under manufacturing and restaurant serving conditions. If the IP proved out, the duration gets extended to long-term under a full licensing agreement with all rights to use the technology.

3. Exclusive versus Non-Exclusive Rights

Just about all the licensing deals I did at the entertainment studios were non-exclusive. Large companies, such as the big toy and apparel companies with the financial resources and who weren't at risk of going under anytime soon, got exclusive deals. These deals included multi-million-dollar guarantees and very aggressive performance milestones (discussed later in this chapter). If they didn't meet their performance milestones, they lost their exclusive rights.

An exclusive license means all your eggs are in one basket. You are relying on one licensee to make all the money with your IP. On the other hand, a non-exclusive license gives you the option to license other companies and receive multiple royalty payments.

Granting exclusive rights doesn't mean giving everything to one partner. It can be broad, such as any product anywhere in the world, or narrowly defined down to the country, product group, or distribution channel. The boundaries depend on the nature of your IP, the licensee's capabilities, and the customer markets.

Stuffed toys (i.e., plush) was a significant product category for many of the kid's character properties I licensed. If the character was popular, I often licensed exclusively to two different licensees - one for the toy channel and one for the gift channel. In addition to different retail distribution, the quality level for gifts was higher than for toys.

Non-exclusive deals, on the other hand, are less risky and offer flexibility, giving you the option to license other companies for the same products or territories (although it's not advisable to do that). But for licensees, it's less beneficial because it allows other companies to compete directly.

Make sure your agreement is explicit in defining the exclusivity/non-exclusivity terms, so your licensing partner understands what their rights include and don't include.

4. Territories

During my time at the studios, it was rare to grant a worldwide license. The opportunities to exploit a popular kid's property around the world in many territories (countries) and product categories made it impossible for one company to do it all. When a territory was outside the United States, it required specific sales performance dates. If they missed it, they lost the rights to that territory.

Don't make the mistake of including all territories just because a licensing partner wants them. Be specific in listing the territories (however those are defined) and make sure there is a deadline by which your licensing partner must start selling in each territory. Otherwise, you can wind up losing money if your licensing partner doesn't do anything in those markets.

5. Performance Guarantees

All licensing deals are performance based. A performance guarantee payment requires the licensee to guarantee a certain amount of royalty revenue over the course of the licensing term, such as $100,000, $500,000, $2 million, etc.

A performance guarantee works in two ways: one, it makes sure the licensee is going to do what they say they're going to do; two, it guarantees that you will receive a minimum amount of royalties from the licensee during the deal duration. It's an incentive for the licensee to do well to recoup the guarantee.

Generally, the minimum guarantee gets paid over the term of the agreement, such as quarterly. Sometimes there's an upfront payment (usually a percentage of the total) known as an advance against the minimum guarantee. The licensee recoups this advance payment from sales. Every licensing deal I did while at the studios required a performance guarantee to be paid quarterly. In most cases, the upfront payment upon signing was equal to 25% - 30% of the minimum guarantee.

Here's an example of how this works. A million-dollar performance guarantee at a royalty rate of 10% means the licensee will pay that amount regardless of whether they generate $10 million in revenue ($10 million X 10% = $1 million). If a portion of that is paid up front, for example, $100,000, they've "prepaid" the royalties on the first one million dollars in sales.

If the minimum guarantee is small (usually $25,000 or less), the entire amount is paid up front. That is also the case if it's a short-term agreement of six months or one year. Another reason for collecting the entire minimum guarantee upfront is if the company is new, or you think they may not pay as agreed. If it's a non-exclusive deal, and they don't perform, you've at least collected the guarantee and don't have to chase them down for any royalties owed.

Keep in mind that most deals don't get an advance payment, especially if there is still a lot of risk in developing the IP.

6. Royalty Rate and Payments

How often a licensee must report is up to you, and in many cases, depends on their sales cycle. In most agreements, quarterly reporting and payments are standard, but semi-annual or annual are also options. The most crucial point is to make sure it's clear in your agreement how and when your partner must report and pay royalties due. It's also important to detail what information must be included in the royalty statements, such as gross or net sales, return allowances, etc., so you can verify they are paying the correct amount of royalties.

The royalty rate is a formula to calculate the amount of money ("royalties") a licensee will pay the IP owner during the term of the licensing agreement. Be very clear on how the formula calculates the royalty rate. If it's not clear, you'll wind up losing money - case in point. There's a big difference between royalties paid on net versus gross sales. One pays the royalty with no or very limited deductions (such as damaged or returned products), the other pays the royalty after lots of deductions (such as production, advertising, and shipping).

Leaving the royalty rate open to interpretation is one of the biggest reasons why IP owners don't receive their full royalty payments. If it's not defined, you and your partner can wind up disputing the amount of each royalty payment.

7. Quality Control

Quality control is an area where intellectual property owners are very engaged with their licensing partners. Levels of quality control vary with the type of IP. Some examples include a medical technology that requires using a particular laboratory and testing facilities; a service technology requiring the licensee to deliver it at an approved standard; a formulation requiring sourcing quality ingredients to produce the finished product; or a trademarked brand where strict QC monitoring and approval for every use and at every stage of product development is critical to keeping the trademark value intact.

Quality control was one of the essential terms in the licensing deals I did while at the studios. The approval process was a non-negotiable term. Licensees had to adhere to a very strict QC program, requiring approvals at every stage of the production process - from concept development to the first productions sample. In many cases, it was a four or five step process that required several months, depending on the licensee's product. The agreements even specified no response means it's not approved until it's approved in writing. That way, the studio ensured it had the time to review and verify all the submissions, and it wouldn't lose control of licensed products in the retail market.

8. Right to Audit

Don't overlook this clause in your licensing agreements. It gives you (the IP owner) the right to check the licensee's books to make sure they have paid the correct amount of royalty payments.

Big entertainment properties with lots of licensees required constant auditing of the licensees, especially if the property was red hot, with dozens of licensees producing hundreds of products. In most cases, licensees were reporting their correct royalties. But there were instances where the audit turned up tens of thousands of dollars in royalties owed (as well as products that weren't in their licensing agreement).

Sometimes royalty calculations are simple, such as for a single product. In other cases, it's complicated, such as a worldwide license with many products and territories. If that's the case, be sure to hire a professional firm that specializes in these types of audits. It helps you keep up licensee control and ensures you are getting paid the royalties owed.

9. Termination

Getting out of the agreement is just as important as getting in. Most of the time, contracts end without any disputes. But if there is a dispute, it's clear how to resolve the dispute. That's the importance of well-defined termination clauses.

I consulted an inventor of a patented accessory item for trucks. Ultimately, they didn't hire me and instead decided to license it themselves. They wound up signing a horrible licensing agreement with a company founded by their former CFO. But they got lucky. The licensee failed to meet the performance clause, and they were able to terminate the licensing agreement and regain control of their IP.

The termination clauses ensure that everybody adheres to the agreement and does what they're supposed to do. They detail what happens if you or your licensing partner doesn't do something you agreed to do. If that happens, there are specific actions to take to fix it. If the issue isn't corrected within the period, such as thirty days, then the agreement can end.

Some of the most common termination causes are failing to meet a performance clause, such as a sales date or development deadline. Others include failing to pay royalties on time, not using the IP properly, or failing to get quality control approvals. They're designed to keep everybody on track, and in the event, something doesn't work out, it's a clear understanding of how the agreement will end and the intellectual property returned to the IP owner. These are imperative clauses. Pay attention to your termination clauses, because they keep everybody out of trouble and will save you from a lot of time and expense in legal disputes.

Summary of Key Points

Don't shortchange the time it takes to structure the right terms in the licensing agreement. The most important goal of the licensing agreement is to get it done right. "Standard terms" are always modified based on the goals and expectations of you and your partner.

One of the best ways to avoid disputes is making sure the terms of your licensing agreement are precise. Don't just rely on wording such as "best efforts." Include specific requirements, such as spending X amount on advertising, or start selling by Y date.

Every license agreement is unique and should reflect the goals and expectations of both you and your licensing partner. You must take the time to make sure your contract terms are clear about the agreed upon responsibilities, milestones, and compliance requirements to avoid future problems. Otherwise, your IP winds up languishing because your licensing partner fails to support your IP as promised, costing you revenues, missed market opportunities, and legal fees trying to unwind the licensing agreement.

Work with a qualified licensing attorney. They will make sure all the agreement terms are clear, your IP rights are protected, and nothing is open to "interpretation" by you or your licensing partner.

CHAPTER 16

Get a Licensing Professional on Your Team

I often meet inventors who have companies interested in licensing their IP, but because their mindset was in "fear" mode, they failed to take any action with these companies. Eventually, these potential partners lost interest, and some big money-making opportunities slipped away.

Getting professional advice from a licensing agent or consultant (such as me) is the best way to "overcome" the fear of the unknown. Their expertise and knowledge licensing will help you manage and make money with your IP. They help you expand your business in new parts of the world and advise on the best way to approach these markets.

An agent provides critical licensing services including identifying new business opportunities, conducting due diligence on potential licensees, ensuring compliance with contract terms, facilitating the transfer of IP assets, monitoring quality control, and collecting royalty payments due.

A licensing agent speeds up the licensing process because they will know which companies will be best suited for (and interested in) the IP. Licensing agents also provide consulting services to help you develop and position your IP, so it's attractive to potential licensees.

When I work with a new client, one of the first things I do is figure out what makes their IP an excellent licensing opportunity. Does it do something better, faster or cheaper, solve a big problem, lower liability costs, or increase profits? Whatever it is, that is what I focus on when first presenting the IP to potential licensing partners. One of my clients created a diabetes education program that solved a big problem - patient compliance in reducing their diabetes risk factors. What made it an even more attractive licensing opportunity is it worked - it had a very high completion rate and documented research showing a significant reduction of patient's diabetes symptoms.

If you are new to licensing or don't have the expertise, or industry relationships, a licensing agent can save you time, money, and resources. If you are not familiar with the licensing process or you don't want to manage your licensing program, then you'll want to consider using a licensing agent. Although an agent adds to the cost of a licensing program, they bring experience, know-how, and resources. They have the professional licensing expertise, knowledge, and skills you need to license your IP.

The Agent Negotiating Advantage

I always recommend using a licensing agent to negotiate your licensing deals. It's one of the best ways to make sure it's a successful negotiation. The biggest reason you should not negotiate on your behalf is you lack objectivity. If you spend years developing your IP, you're emotionally invested, and you take critical questions during the negotiations personally. A licensing agent is objective and focuses on bringing the negotiation to a successful conclusion.

I've seen this situation many times, especially with inventors. Most often, they don't have a realistic opinion of the value of their IP. They think it's worth millions, yet it still hasn't been market tested or received regulatory approval. When they don't get an offer they like, they get insulted and walk away. Or worse, they don't understand what they are negotiating and wind up agreeing to terms that aren't in their best interest.

Working with an IP Attorney and a Licensing Agent

It's important that the attorney and agent work together and understand each other's role. An attorney reviews and prepares licensing documents, and provides basic legal advice on IP rights. A licensing agent will typically focus on finding licenses and negotiating the deals.

Here are some tips on how to work with your IP attorney and licensing agent:

- The agent answers general questions about licensing terms or royalty rates.

- The agent should have a form agreement that he uses as the starting point in any negotiation.

- Before the agent offers a licensing agreement to any potential licensees, the attorney should check it to make sure that it represents the IP Owners' interests.

- If a licensee provides their licensing agreement, the agent should do the negotiating and then have the attorney review it before signing it.

- After signing the licensing agreement, the agent manages the licensee relationship, from providing information about the IP, making sure the licensee is performing, to collecting royalty payments.

- If a licensee has breached the license agreement in a minor way, such as by making a royalty payment ten days late, the agent handles it.

- If the licensee stops performing or doesn't correct a minor breach, the attorney determines the options available and guidance on how to resolve the issues.

The amount of expert help you will need also evolves. At the beginning of the process, it may only be one licensing partner. Over time, your licensing program grows, and as you approach the deal-making stage, you'll need a team consisting of an attorney and licensing professional to manage and navigate the deals with partners in different industries and companies. Managing and using the team efficiently helps you get the most money from your licensing program.

Licensing Agent Agreements

Licensing agents work in several ways. The most common are contingency and retainer-based. Contingency means they only get paid if they get a licensing deal. Most contingency licensing agents will want exclusivity, meaning they are the only agent who can represent your IP. Commissions generally average between 30% and 40% of gross licensing revenue and may run as high as 50%. Contingent agents often represent lots of different intellectual properties, so the time spent focusing your IP may be limited.

Retainer based agents will work exclusively and non-exclusively. Generally, they'll require a minimum monthly retainer plus a percentage commission on each licensing deal. The commission is usually lower than contingent agents but not always. Since they are retainer-based, they typically have fewer clients and spend more time focusing on each licensing campaign. (By the way, I am a retainer-based agent).

With both types of agents, you'll have to pay other expenses such as trade show costs, travel costs, and legal fees.

Some licensing agents require a minimum term of two or three years since it often takes that long to find licensees and begin to receive royalties. Also, an agent will want an option to renew or extend the agreement, usually a month to month or for an extended term. Typical renewal options include automatic renewal, mutually agreed to, or performance-based where the agent achieves a certain amount of royalty income.

If the agent agreement term ends (and is not renewed) or terminates early, you still have to pay commissions to the agent. That includes all licensing deals completed and in "active negotiation" that close within a particular time, such as six months after the termination. Renewals and extensions are often paid at a reduced commission rate and can include a sliding scale (e.g., 40% for the first year after termination, 30% for the second year, and 20% for the remaining years).

Licensing agents (and most licensees) rarely get involved with raw idea or concepts that are unprotected and untested. An intellectual property still in the idea stage is the wrong time to seek out a licensing agent. These idea concepts have little or no value. The right time to approach the licensing agent is with a ready-to-go IP that has the necessary research to back up its real value.

Patent Broker vs. Licensing Agent

I'll wrap up this chapter with a quick summary of patent brokers vs. licensing agents. The big difference is patent brokers focus on finding buyers and not licensees. But unlike licensing agents, patent brokers also work both on the sell and buy side of the transaction. On the sell side, they estimate the patent's value and market potential to figure a price. On the buyer side, patent brokers help buyers find patents, evaluate patent risk, and decide a fair buying price.

The engagement term with a patent broker is shorter. After completing the patent sale, they receive a success fee, usually a percentage of the selling price, and the engagement ends. They don't participate in the recurring revenue from licensing deals. On the buy side, the engagement continues until the client completes the purchase of one or more patents.

If you're interested in using a patent broker, research them online and contact them directly to find out about their services and fees.

Summary of Key Points

If you are new to licensing, don't want to manage it yourself, or don't have the experience or industry relationships, then a licensing agent is right for you.

An agent gives you an experienced IP "professional" to offer you hands-on advice on how to effectively maneuver all of your licensing activities. Their ability and knowledge of the licensing business will help you make the most money with your IP. They speed up the licensing process and more importantly, they'll be objective in the negotiations, have more negotiating experience and will keep you out of trouble

112

Get a Licensing Professional on Your Team

Although an agent adds to the cost of a licensing program, they're experience, know-how and resources will save you a lot of time and money in the long-run. Before engaging a consultant or agent, do thorough due diligence on them and make sure you understand what they will do and how they will get compensated.

CHAPTER 17

There Are No Boundaries

Here's one of the most exciting things about licensing: it's a growing global marketplace where your intellectual property can be used simultaneously by many partners in multiple products, industries, and territories.

IP is in demand everywhere, and licensing is now a strategy being used more often by companies large and small, whether it's expanding distribution, finding new customers, tapping partner's resources, or accessing money by generating more revenues.

Many countries that, just a decade ago, were not active in developing intellectual property, are now becoming new markets for licensing intellectual property. Although IP laws vary from country to country, the process of licensing - the money-making side - operates in the same way.

Government resources are also similar. For example, in the U.S., it is the Patent and Trademark Office (USPTO) and the Copyright Office. In other countries, you'll find similar types of government organizations, such as the China Patent Office (CNIPA) and the European Patent Office (EPO). All of these government bodies support the development, protection, and commercialization of intellectual property.

Even licensing agreements have become standardized to a certain extent. Today, all types of licensing agreements for patents, trademarks, and copyrights are similar in terms and used in multiple countries. I've worked with many licensing agreements that were the same format for Europe and the U.S. This is one of the big reasons why licensing operates just about the same anywhere in the world.

Entertainment is an excellent example of global licensing. Popular kid's properties reach countries around the world and create licensing opportunities in just about every consumer product category. I did license deals with companies in many different countries including toys, apparel and video games, and in some cases, simultaneously to several companies in the same product category.

International Licensing Strategies

Licensing is a low-risk and low-cost way to plant your flag internationally. It's an especially good strategy if you're a startup or small business with limited financial resources.

Licensing offers several strategies for entering international markets. Which one you use depends on your IP and business goals. Direct licensing, cross-licensing and sub-licensing are three of the most common strategies. What works for one type of IP doesn't necessarily work for every IP.

In most cases, it starts with marketing your IP successfully in your home market. Success there is a good sign that it could work well internationally. Some technologies are easier than others, particularly those integrated into global products, such as smartphones and computers.

Tapping local licensing partner's resources - sales, distribution, production, and marketing - is one of the fastest and lowest-risk ways to enter a foreign market. Licensing a bigger international partner is also a great strategy to keep your IP rights intact, especially in a country or region with weak IP laws. Licensing limits your investment risk by partnering with companies in local markets with the know-how, customer base, and established distribution channels.

It's also a strategy for getting into markets where direct ownership is not an option. A good example is China. Because local laws prohibit 100% ownership by foreign companies, licensing is an ideal strategy for this territory. It's a rapidly expanding consumer market, with 300 million middle-class consumers, spending on everything from branded apparel to cars, computers, and more.

Many of the world's largest corporations in the computer, pharmaceutical, entertainment, consumer products, and other industries use licensing to build and expand their international marketplace. Some of the companies generating one billion dollars or more in global licensing revenues include IBM, Texas Instruments, Qualcomm, Microsoft, and Ericsson.

4 Tips for Finding an International Partner

Here are some pointers to consider when searching for international licensing partners:

1. Do Your Homework: Before entering a foreign market, do your homework and find out who the leading players are in each market. Try to meet your prospective licensee in person, such as at an international trade show, which is a great way to learn about the markets and meet potential licensing candidates. While phone, video call, and email are what's used most of the time,

establishing a personal relationship is essential since your licensing agreement will run for a couple of years or longer.

2. The Right Partner is Key: Your partner is the most crucial part of an international licensing agreement. If your partner doesn't have the right capabilities to get your IP into the marketplace, it can damage your IP value or worse; you may wind up losing control of your IP rights - especially if it's in an emerging market where the IP laws are not as mature. That's why it's critical to research your potential partner. Time spent doing a good job of due diligence (as I discussed in an earlier chapter) will save you lots of time and money trying to get out of a bad partnership, as well as reduce the risk of damaging your IP.

3. Be Flexible on the Royalty Rate. What works in one country may not work in another due to production costs, lower profit margins, or changing economic conditions. I was managing the licensing program in Mexico for one of the big kid's properties. At that time the studio contracted with a local licensing agent to work with local licensees. All the licensing agreements were payable in dollars. Since the dollar/peso exchange rate had been stable for quite some time, it wasn't an issue. Shortly after the licensing program was up and running, the Mexican economy suddenly took a nose dive. The peso dropped in value like a lead balloon, and overnight, the royalties owed quadrupled based on the value of the peso to the dollar. To solve the problem and keep the Mexico licensing program intact and profitable, we came up with a formula for recalculating the royalties with a "new" exchange rate.

4. Start Short-Term: If a potential partner is new to an industry, but they are a company you'd like to work with,

consider doing a short-term agreement. You can learn about their capabilities, such as the strength of their distribution into different countries or whether they can successfully produce your product at a competitive price, before committing to a long-term licensing agreement. I used this strategy with one of my clients. They introduced their new invention at a big trade show and got immediate interest from an international distributor. We structured a two-part deal. First, as a distributor to test the market, and based on the sales success, it was expanded to a long-term licensing agreement with rights to make and sell the product in Europe.

What to Watch Out For

As far as the legal pitfalls go, some of the biggest ones to watch out for are not having a clear understanding of the local market laws, not protecting your IP internationally, and signing a poorly structured licensing agreement.

Before signing any licensing agreement, be sure to check it with a qualified attorney who knows the local market laws. Make sure your licensing agreement is very clear about royalty payments, development milestones, performance benchmarks and, most important, IP control (registering and maintaining your IP rights in foreign markets), so you don't wind up trying to settle a dispute in an international court.

Summary of Key Points

Today every IP owner must think globally. Before licensing out internationally, you'll need to decide if you want to run internationally. If so, it requires protecting and managing your IP globally.

There Are No Boundaries

As the global licensing marketplace expands, in many ways, it's becoming easier to develop business outside your home country. Working directly with a company outside the United States is an excellent licensing strategy, simply because that company is already established there, as opposed to working with a U.S. company to try to open that foreign territory. The same holds for a foreign IP owner looking to enter the US market.

Expanding internationally through licensing is a great way to capture new growth opportunities with less risk. Licensing lets you quickly tap into your partners' resources and market experience. You can start small - for example, licensing your IP to one licensing partner in one market. As your licensing revenues grow, international licensing gives you the flexibility to add more licensing partners or sell directly.

Intellectual property and licensing works the same, whether you are in Toledo or Tokyo. Today, the Internet enables anybody to license anywhere in the world without having to travel physically. Most of the international deals I do via conference call and email. And you can do the same thing. With the right kind of IP, you could be receiving cash flow from all around the world.

CHAPTER 18

Licensing is a Two-Way Street

Although this book focuses on licensing out from the IP owners' perspective, keep in mind that licensing is a two-way street. The other side is in-licensing. The most significant advantage of in-licensing market ready IP is it saves development time and costs, letting you focus your resources on what you do best - selling and making money with your products or services.

Why Licensing In is a Great Strategy

Industries such as computers, electronics, consulting, consumer products, and more are shifting to the licensing model. Many of the world's biggest companies not only license out their IP but also use licensing to develop new products and services.

In-licensing a market-ready IP minimizes the risks of developing it yourself and shortens the time to market. It saves you lots of time and money in R&D costs. Rather than spending money and time to develop a new IP internally, you find one that's market ready, and license rights to make and sell it. The IP owners have tested and protected it. They'll often provide their know-how and expertise on the best way to produce it or make it better.

In-licensing is also a great strategy to differentiate your product in the market, especially if it's a "commodity." While I was at the studios, I licensed one of the big kid's summer movies to a small bike company. Bikes, especially for little kids, are a low-cost, low margin commodity product in a very competitive and promotions intensive market. This company was struggling against major manufacturers. They were looking for a way to differentiate their bikes, to sell more, and gain exposure at retail. Their goal was to get into the big mass market retailers. They developed a bike featuring the character colors and included all sorts of character-related accessories (horns, bike stickers, etc.). When the movie opened, they were the only "movie-branded bike," and their sales skyrocketed. They got orders from every mass market retailer scrambling to fill their shelves as demand for movie-related products soared.

If you are competing in a "commodity" business, licensing differentiates your product. And if it's the right license, your sales can skyrocket. Plus, you get the added benefit of the licensor's resources, including access to new technologies, high brand visibility, retail shelf space, consumer recognition, and promotional muscle.

Market ready IP gives you an immediate market presence. A big licensing partner wants you to succeed, and you can tap their resources, such as manufacturing and distribution. Often, licensing is used to tap into a partner's promotional power. The strategy is called "Riding the Coattails," and it's used to multiply your promotional dollars without spending more money. By partnering with a big IP owner, such as a major consumer brand, you can leverage their promotional power to enhance the visibility of your product or service in the market.

I used this strategy with a client who invented a new portable "bar and grill entertainment center" that was ideal for tailgating. Rather than spending all their money to try to promote it "generically," I helped them license several big college and professional football team brands. They "branded" their product with team logos and colors, and got immediate access to the big retailers, instant customer recognition, and promotional support from the televised football games, and multiple "brand" promotions from the other licensing partners.

Building market awareness and consumer demand in this day and age is a costly undertaking, especially if you are a small company or start-up with limited resources. If you are looking for a way to get promotional muscle behind your products or services, then licensing a well-known brand could be the right licensing strategy for you.

Some IP has the potential to grow your business from zero to millions of dollars overnight. One example of this is entertainment content, particularly for kids. When these properties suddenly become popular among kids, the demand for products skyrockets. I saw this first hand when I was licensing some of the biggest kid's entertainment properties. When demand exploded, companies who licensed these properties were generating millions of dollars in sales. Some of them reached this level of sales in less than two years from the time they got the license.

And it wasn't just established companies. One licensee was a husband-and-wife team who got in before the TV show became a huge hit. They got rights to use the characters on several small household products. Eighteen months later, their sales exceeded $10 million, and they paid over $1 million in royalties. Several companies went public and saw their IPO skyrocket as a result of having the license.

While this is the exception, it is a good illustration of the potential "business growth power" of licensing. Getting rights to intellectual property is a strategy many businesses often overlook, yet it's a great way to build your business.

Where to Find IP to License

There is an abundance of market-ready IP available from large corporations, universities, and research labs. Visit the websites of many largest corporations, and you'll find a list of IP available for licensing. They've got large patent portfolios, and they license out the ones they are not using. Many universities have lots of intellectual property available for licensing as well. In particular, they look for startups to develop and get the IP into the marketplace. Some Universities offer other resources, such as office and research facilities, and sometimes access to potential funding sources. Government agencies, such as defense, agriculture, and space, are also resources of IP. They create these technologies for use by the government, and they also license it out to companies for the commercial market.

Many great licensing opportunities are also found using inside sources such as industry trade events, investment conferences, and trade shows (such as the Licensing Show, CES, IMPEX, and others). If you are new to licensing or don't have the ability (or relationships), this is where licensing agents and consultants (such as myself) can help.

It takes time to find the right IP and licensing opportunity. It requires you to be active in the market. Some of my clients hire me as their "eyes and ears" and help them find IP to license in. Entertainment properties are one example. I've worked with several clients who wanted to license popular movie franchises. These are tough IPs to license because they're often locked up in long-term license deals between the studios and large manufacturers. But sometimes we were there at the right time, and licensed rights to a new product category or territory that was opening up.

The best approach is to understand what type of IP you are searching for, such as a new patented consumer product, technology, or a big brand. Knowing what you are looking for makes the search process more efficient and improves the chances of finding (and getting) the right IP.

The Three Most Important Questions

Licensing in the right type of intellectual property can be a fast track to the commercial marketplace. But if you fail to ask the right questions, you can wind up with an IP that costs you more than just a licensing fee.

When you're looking to license in an IP, the first thing you must do is verify the IP owners do own the IP. Do your homework. If it's a patent, do a patent search to confirm its ownership, all the maintenance fees are current, and there are no infringement actions. Before licensing a brand, make sure it's registered for the products or services you're seeking to license, and the IP owner isn't in dispute with a licensee or someone else.

Second is to understand what rights are in the license. If it's a patent, what is the technology and does it require know-how? For example, a new patent product requires the manufacturing know-how to produce it. If this know-how isn't part of the rights, you'll be unable to make and sell it. If it's a movie or a TV show, does it include the use of character or celebrity images? If you don't find out precisely what IP rights are included, you can wind up missing the most critical parts for commercial success.

The third is what the licensor expects of you as a licensee. Are you going to be on your own or will the IP owner offer support? You must understand this. For example, if you do a licensing deal with a major studio or big brand, sometimes they'll give you support, and sometimes they won't. You must consider this. Is it a brand or an IP that you can get to market on your own, or do you need some support?

One of my clients faced this issue when we licensed one of the big auto brands. The agent representing it told us: "The licensor offers no support. You're on your own. Here's the license. There's no advertising, no promotion, no nothing." We were surprised the licensor didn't offer any retail support, such as buyer introductions, or a coordinated retail program for cross promotions with the brand. But their position was that the brand was so big and well-known, they didn't have to offer anything beyond the license rights.

That's an example of what can occur. It's a critical issue you must consider before going forward with the licensing agreement - particularly if you have limited financial resources to develop and market the IP.

Summary of Key Points

You don't have to reinvent the wheel when it comes to developing new products and technologies. Licensing in a market-tested and ready to go IP is one of the fastest ways to get a new product or technology into the market. It reduces one of the biggest and costly risks (R&D) and lets you focus all of your money, people, and resources on marketing and selling the product or technology.

Billions of dollars of IP is sitting on the books of corporations, universities, research labs, and government agencies around the world. These are sources of available intellectual property and a goldmine of licensing opportunities waiting to be mined by startups and small businesses. Any of this IP could develop into a lucrative licensing opportunity.

Before signing the agreement, make sure you verify the IP ownership, rights included, and what type of support the IP owner will offer.

Licensing is a dynamic process that requires you to be active in the market and making it part of your daily business activities. Remember, the best licensing opportunities go to those that make licensing a part of their short and long-term strategy.

CHAPTER 19

The Sky's the Limit

We live in exciting times. It is very challenging to launch a new IP by starting a business. At the same time, the challenge opens up a lot of opportunities, especially for new IP. Innovation is in its heyday. In turn, one of the nicest things about intellectual property is that there are no limitations to it. IP is an infinite resource that exists all around us.

Over the last decade, there is study after study is confirming the wealth-creating power of IP rights. It is the driver of economic growth, incomes, jobs, investment, and trade. Licensing opportunities are all around you. And they will continue growing over the coming years as the economies of the world change.

Keep in mind that ideas by themselves have very little value. A lot of people have a lot of ideas, but they don't have much value unless you do something with them. However, once you turn an idea into intellectual property, you can then use licensing to change it into an economic asset that generates revenues on a variety of levels.

Licensing is the process that turns innovative IP into income producing opportunities. It allows you to leverage your inventions, technologies, know-how, formulas, core competencies, customers, revenues, markets, distribution - any and everything that solves problems and creates value. By understanding what licensing is and how to use it, you can capitalize on your IP to create all types of income-producing opportunities.

In today's market, you can make more money from licensing your IP than from selling a product or service. Often a little creative exploration can discover new uses and applications for your IP beyond its current product or technology form. Think of it this way. It's the difference between earning income by selling just one type of product and creating wealth by generating revenue from two, three, four or more licensing partners selling multiple products, uses or applications of your IP simultaneously.

The Next Step is Up to You

I wrote this book to get you started and show you the way, but ultimately, the weight is on your shoulders. It only takes one deal - the right deal - to make a lot of money with licensing. But you must take action. One of the biggest challenges is not taking action with IP. That's why 95% of intellectual property doesn't make money.

Timing is everything, and in a dynamic market, what's cold today can become red-hot tomorrow. The most important part of the licensing process is to keep it going. It's not the best IP that makes money; it's the best-marketed IP that makes money. You can't be the first to market if you never start the race.

The rules of licensing are simple. They are like a formula. It's a process that requires taking specific action steps that transform your IP from an intangible asset into money-making products, services, and technologies. It's a creative process limited only by your imagination and willingness to collaborate with others to discover what you can do with it. Licensing is a process that, once learned, gives you the unlimited ability to generate wealth with intellectual property.

RESOURCES

About Licensing Consulting Group

Licensing Consulting Group (LCG) specializes in the business development side of IP. Our services focus on one goal: capitalizing on your IP to generate revenue in as many ways as possible. Our role varies, depending on your needs, from a consulting role in IP strategy, to actively managing the licensing program, or operating as a virtual IP team.

LCG's experience includes many types of IP - healthcare technologies, consumer products, entertainment content, product inventions, process technologies, and more. Each IP is unique, and we know how to analyze it, identify the value drivers, and package and license it - whether exclusively to one partner, strategically to select markets, or broadly into multiple product categories.

Whether you are ready to explore new licensing opportunities, get advice on your intellectual property, or looking to optimize your current licensing activities, Licensing Consulting Group helps you capitalize on all your licensing options.

Sign up for our free newsletter at www.licensingcg.com /newsletter.

Website: www.licensingcg.com

Email: info@licensingcg.com

Tel: (646) 395-9572

About Licensing4Profits.com

Licensing4Profits is an online resource offering information, training, and real-world expertise on the licensing processes and how to use it to make money buying and selling intellectual property rights.

L4P provides you with the licensing "know-how" for any stage of the IP licensing process – whether you are new to the world of licensing, ready to take your first step, or need help moving to the next level of your licensing activities.

At Licensing4Profits, you'll get access to blog articles, live workshops, coaching events, webinars, audio and video courses, and continuously updated content with the real world "how-to" actionable information.

Sign up for our free newsletter at www.licensing4profits.com /newsletter.

Website: licensing4proftis.com

Email: info@licensing4profits.com

About The Author

Rand Brenner is CEO of Licensing Consulting Group (LCG) and founder of Licensing4Profits.com. He is an intellectual property professional whose passion is helping inventors, startups, and businesses of all sizes use licensing to transform their IP into money-making products, services, and technologies.

His decades of licensing experience includes a wide range of intellectual property, from healthcare technology to entertainment content, consumer products, software, brands, food, and more. He's licensed some of the biggest Hollywood entertainment blockbusters including the Batman Movies (1 and 2), and the number one kid's action TV show, the Mighty Morphin Power Rangers.

Rand is a featured speaker at investment conferences, trade shows, colleges, and startup events. He's a published writer with articles appearing in several prestigious trade magazine including *The Licensing Journal*, and *Intellectual Property Magazine*. He also mentors at the Cal State Fullerton School of Business and Economics and is a judge for their startup business plan competitions.

Rand received his undergraduate degree in Advertising from California State University - San Jose and his Masters of Business Administration from Pepperdine University.

Made in the USA
Coppell, TX
07 March 2021

51329447R00081